Discover Your Coat Of Many Colors

You Were Born To Be Significant!

FYNE C. OGONOR

Copyright © 2019 Fyne Ogonor.

fyneauthor@gmail.com
www.FyneOgonor.com

All rights reserved. No part of this book may be reproduced, stored, or transmitted by any means—whether auditory, graphic, mechanical, or electronic—without written permission of both publisher and author, except in the case of brief excerpts used in critical articles and reviews. Unauthorized reproduction of any part of this work is illegal and is punishable by law.

Library of Congress Control Number: 2019914765

ISBN:
Paperback: 978-1-951460-00-6
Ebook: 978-1-951460-01-3

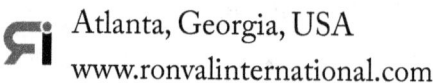

Atlanta, Georgia, USA
www.ronvalinternational.com

Dedication

I dedicate this book, Discover Your Coat of Many Colors, first to my heavenly Father—my Creator and my God. Great is His Faithfulness.

Also, I dedicate this book to my wonderful children, Valerie Uzhiyekachi, Ronald Chiemele, Bryan Chinwuke, Jessica Amanu, and Stephanie Chinem Ogonor. It's a great blessing and privilege to be your mother. For the joy you bring to my heart, may you always experience joy, peace, and happiness, In Jesus' Name. Amen.

In addition to my biological children, I also want to dedicate this book, "Discover Your Coat of Many Colors" to all my spiritual sons and daughters; and to my present and future grandchildren. May the truth and the grace of our Living Savior, and the promises of our God manifest in your lives, to live in abundance of God's blessings; in Jesus precious name. Amen.

Furthermore, I extend the dedication of this book to all that will read this book; may you discover your destiny to live a fruitful and a joy-filled life.
You were born to be significant!

Acknowledgements

I want to thank my daughter, Valerie for typesetting some of this script, and for being there for me whenever I called on her on technology matters. I also thank my husband Vincent for his support.

In addition, I want to thank all the Ronval books team members that worked tirelessly to make this book a reality: the editor, the book designers, and everyone who has anything to do with the making of this book. May God bless every one of you in Jesus precious name. Amen.

All glory and adoration I give to my Lord for the inspirations He has given me through the Holy Spirit. I especially thank God for assuring me with promises I can always count on, because He is always able to carry me through.

Special Recognition:
Profile picture: by my son, Ronald Ogonor.
Thank you, and may God bless your endeavors. IJN. Amen.

Contents

Preface
The Beginning of a Journey 8

Part One
You were Born with a Heritage

Chapter One : Be Accountable For Your Life 14

Chapter Two : Know Your Heritage and Possess It 18

Chapter Three : Why God Shields Your Identity 30

Part Two
Life Reflections

Chapter Four : The Quest Of Life 44

Part Three
Battling With The Feeling Of Inadequacy

Chapter Five : Are you afraid of your call? 64

Part Four
Destiny Awaits!

Chapter Six : Why Am I Here? 82

Chapter Seven : Experiencing The Illogical 88

Chapter Eight : The Voice Of Destiny 100

Part Five
Demolish Evil Foundation & Build On The Rock

Chapter Nine : What Is Your Foundation? 124

Chapter Ten : Understanding The Principles Of Life .. 144

Part Six
Blessing The Children

Chapter Eleven : My Beloved 158

Part Seven
Acknowledge God!

Chapter Twelve : The Songs Of My Heart 176

Chapter Thirteen : The Bottom Line 188

Preface

The Beginning of a Journey

In every journey, there is a starting point and an ending point. And in-between, you'll experience different things. While in transit, we hope for the best experience; however, our experiences are not always pleasant because the world is full of the good, the bad, and the ugly. How we react to these experiences is completely our decision. Also, there is no one destination for every journey. You decide where you're going before you start. You control the why, when, how and where; the starting point and the ending point. But what happens in-between is beyond your control, for such is known only by your creator.

Our life's journey is similar to what I've just described, because of the battle between good and evil. However, in life's journey, the master planner, the creator, is the originator and the terminator; and He laid down a perfect plan, with a predestined destination. A plan that included every creature on earth. A plan of eternal heritage; for humans, one people, one purpose, and one destination-life eternal. But our enemy, the liar, the deceiver, the old serpent, took away that privilege from us. As a result, the destination our creator had designed for us multiplied; we now have more than one destination. Our creator, however, redeemed our original prepackaged destiny, but He gives us a choice to reshape it to whatever we want, out of love. Even at that, He desires us to make the right decision by choosing what He wants for us; for all His plans for us are good.

Due to what the enemy did to mankind, the human race now faces the challenge of identifying the simple things of life, which has been made complex by error, such as identity and purpose, which are instrumental to finding our destiny. Hence, we have questions like, "Why Am I Here?" This question addresses the purpose, the mission of our being on planet Earth. Let's explore together to understand the true meaning of life, and how to identify our individual destiny through human drives. What does life mean to you?

My Coat of Many Colors

I woke up from what I thought was a nightmare,
And I found myself wearing a coat of many colors.
"A coat of many colors," is a multiple blessing from God.
A coat of many colors sometimes seems like a curse,
And sometimes it is difficult to meet the challenges that come with the coat of many colors.
It attracts enemies; it attracts friends.
Come what may, the coat of many colors is
a message to the world.
A message to a diverse universe,
One people, different tongues.
A coat of many colors,
The abundance of God's blessings;
That, I shall wear.

PART ONE

You Were Born With A Heritage

> ¹ *In the beginning God created the heavens and the earth.*
> ² *The earth was without form, and void; and darkness was on the face of the deep. And the Spirit of God was hovering over the face of the waters.*
> Genesis 1: 1-2, NKJV.

Dream

Dream! is as big as you can imagine it.
Dream big and achieve big.
Small dreams limit your success;
Bigger dreams widen your vision,
and expand your knowledge.
Dream it, and you can imagine it.
Imagine it, and you can perceive it.
Visualize it, and you can achieve it.
Achievement is success,
and success is progress.
Progress begets recognition,
acceptance, and visibility.
Dreaming the big dreams, is honorable.

-*"A Moving Train" by Fyne C. Ogonor*

CHAPTER ONE

Be Accountable For Your Life

Find Answers to Your Who, Why, How And Your What?

In order for you to be accountable for your life, you must take cognizance of the following:
- You must know who you are, the Real you.
- You must know and understand that you were born with a heritage.
- You must be able to identify what life means to you.

This book, *Discover Your Coat of Many Colors*, is designed to provide answers to the most important questions for every human being; to understand the true meaning of life; and how to get to your divine destination. Some of those questions are:

- Who Am I?
- Whom do I belong to?
- How did I get here?
- Why Am I here?
- What Can I do? And
- What is my destiny?

Knowing the answers to these basic questions will help you understand the significance of your existence on planet Earth. I.e., what your life is all about.

Also, Discover Your Coat of Many Colors, reveals the blessings of God, and how to position yourself to receive God's blessings, standing on His promises. In a nutshell, it is a book for dreamers without limit; those who aspire to achieve and succeed beyond all odds; yet, retain peace, joy and happiness, the benefits of true success.

Every outstanding dream or vision must generate both friends and enemies. In any case, the dreamer's eyes should always be focused on Him who brings our dreams to reality, the Almighty God. No matter what you do, enemies will always try to pull you down through discouragement, envy, jealousy, and hatred, even when there is no wrong doing on your part.

But the important thing is staying focused and looking up for help. In the end, it is what God says that must be the bottom line. Moreover, remain in God's presence, and in His plan always, for victory assurance.

Why do you care so much about the validation of your identity by others while they do not know the real you inside?

As you read this book, receive and claim the blessings and the promises of God by faith, and it will work for you. Also, take the divine instructions of wisdom, apply them into your life, then watch and see the wonders of God manifesting with an overflowing harvest in your life. For Jehovah has pronounced you kings/queens and priests; and commanded you to subdue and take dominion over the earth. Now, get up and take what belongs to you. It is your heritage.

Read this book and remain blessed.

CHAPTER TWO

Know Your Heritage, And Possess It

"In the beginning was the Word, and the Word was with God, and the Word was God. 2 He was in the beginning with God. 3 All things were made through Him, and without Him nothing was made that was made." John 1:1-3 NKJV

Then God said, "Let Us make man in Our image, according to Our likeness; let them have dominion over the fish of the sea, over the birds of the air, and over the cattle, over [g]all the earth and over every creeping thing that creeps on the earth." 27 So God created man in His own image; in the image of God He created him; male and female He created them. 28 Then God blessed them, and God said to them, "Be fruitful and multiply; fill the earth and subdue it; have dominion over the fish of the sea, over the birds of the air, and over every living thing that [h]moves on the earth." Genesis 1:26-28 NKJV

Knowing your identity starts from the passages above; they answered all the important questions of life as mentioned previously. If you have not understood up to now how you came to be, and your mission, what I'm about to present to you now should enlighten you further.

The questions of life:
- Who Am I? And Whom do I belong to? These two questions deal with your Identity, and your Heritage.
- Why Am I here? And What can I do? These questions deal with the Purpose of life, your mission, and your potentials.
- Here I Am; How did I get here? Is the question of Recognition or Acceptance.
- What is my Destination? This deals with your Security, and your Destiny, the End Result.

Identity
Who Are You?
Who Am I?

I'll like to start with the story of a young boy named David. In the eyes of human beings, he was known as an animal keeper, a shepherd boy, taking care of the lambs and sheep in the bush. The least among his siblings, and in the eyes of his father. In the eyes of God, he was a shepherd of human flocks, a defender of his people, a mighty warrior, a King, a child of the Almighty God, a worshipper, and a man after God's own heart.

At David's very young age, God sent Prophet Samuel to anoint David as a King to rule over his people. When the prophet got to Bethlehem, he invited Jesse to come to a festival with all his sons. Knowing the importance of the prophet's mission, Mr. Jesse hurriedly gathered his seven big boys and headed for the party. At the party, Jesse introduced his sons one by one to prophet Samuel to locate the one to be anointed. Initially, from their physique, their outward appearance, the Prophet was certain it had to be one of them. After he had seen all present, so he could identify who among them was to be anointed King, according to God's instructions. The Lord told him that the one to be anointed wasn't there.

As he could not find the one, he was looking for, he asked their father, Jesse, "are these all the sons you have?" He said yes, these are all my big boys because Jesse was judging with his human logic. The prophet shook his head and said, no, the one I'm looking for is not here, he knew God never makes mistakes. He asked Mr. Jesse again, are you sure these are the only boys you have? Jesse put his hand on his chain, rubbed his lap and said, well, there is the least among them in the field watching the flocks, I know it cannot be him; he's just a little boy, he's not a King material. He's the least among them.

Hearing about this very young and unfit boy, according to his family; the prophet requested to see David regardless. "Can you bring him to me?" And immediately Prophet Samuel saw David, he said, "this is the one the Lord has chosen to be anointed King over Israel". And he anointed David as the new King of Israel, to take over rulership of Israel from Saul. David's family members underestimated him. They marveled with amazement because they were oblivious of David's value, and his spiritual worth. They were incognizant of the real identity of their brother and son, David. Obviously, he was more of God's son than he was Jesse's; therefore, his family could not identify with him in the supernatural state.

Wow! The least among men is now the highest according to God's plan. Amazing!

The Giant was Slain
Identity is a simple word, yet very complex to interpret.

Psychology taught me that identity is a characteristic component that makes up an individual. In other words, identity is the projection of the "Self," the "I, or Me" both inward and outward personality. Because of its psychological complexity, it is better to align your thinking of understanding the real you, from the viewpoint of your maker, the Creator. This is because, the Real You is the spirit being that inhabits the body, forms a soul, and lives inside your designed body by God,{the temple, or house}.

The reasons you must study your identity from your maker's point of view are as follows:
- Your human understanding of who you are, is often different from what others think, and sometimes contrary to the real you.

- Others' perception of who you are, often contradict the real you; this is because they cannot see the real you inside of you. They can only know of your outward personality and experience your expression from your innerself through communication. However, their judgement of who you are based on the above points depends on their own perception, their understanding, which is influenced by their belief system.

- Sometimes, God shields the understanding of your true or real identity to protect you. Especially if He had created you to fulfill an uncommon assignment. He shields you, so the enemy will not discover you too soon before God equips you in the field—before the battles come against you.

Chapter 2: Know your heritage and possess it

Have you ever ventured in a dream bigger than yourself? Meaning, the dream is so big that people feel it is beyond your capacity; even when you are succeeding, people around you would keep discouraging you, telling you to tone it down. They would say things like:
--You are setting up yourself for failure,
--Why do you think you can do that?
-- Why don't you stay in your Comfort zone, etc.?

In 1st Samuel chapter 17, this is what happened to David. The same David that was anointed earlier. Again, his abilities were underrated by his siblings, his king, Saul, and the armies, especially by Goliath, the Philistine giant.

One day, David's father, Jesse called out David from the field where he was caring for the flocks of sheep and gave him food and drink for his first three sons. David's three oldest brothers were in the battlefield in the valley of Ellah where the Israelite army camped for their battle against the Philistines. David was also to check on how they were faring, so he could bring a report to the father on the status of the battle.

Upon David's arrival, he saw their army marching into the battlefield singing war songs. He dropped his belongings with the supplies keeper and ran towards the battlefield to inquire of his brothers. As he proceeded closer, he witnessed a giant from the Philistine army boasting and challenging the Israelite's army asking them as he had been doing for days, as he was told, to bring a man to challenge him. If he kills the man, all Israel would become slaves to serve the Philistines. But, if the man kills him, they would be slaves and serve the Israelites.

As David heard the giant's threats, his heart rumbled with anger because he sensed great fear among the Israelites army. David mingled among their army inquiring of this giant with a fowl mouth called Goliath. At this time, David was told of King Saul's vow; the King promised to give great wealth to whoever kills this giant that was defiling the Israelites. Also, that the King will give such a man his daughter in marriage. In addition, he would exempt his family from paying taxes. Again, David asked another man, what will be the reward of whoever kills this giant and removes shame and disgrace from the face of Israel? The man answered David as the first man about King Saul's vow.

As David listened to this giant, the anger in his heart started growing, and he said, "who is this uncircumcised, Philistine that he should defy the armies of the living God?" As Aliab, his oldest brother noticed David communicating with the men, he became very furious at David, asking, "what brought you to the battlefield? "Why have you come down here? And who did you leave those few sheep in the wilderness with?" His elder brother continued, "I know how your mind operates, your inquisitive mind has compelled you to come and watch the battle; "I know that's why you have come."

David responded, what have I done wrong now? Can't I talk to people? Hey, big Brother, calm down! I'm just socializing with these men to lift their spirit, to release the tension about the battle. Okay! After the above interrogation, David turned to another man and asked the same question again. Still, he was given the same answer as before about the king's promise. Then David reacted with a sarcastic comment about killing the giant. Whatever he said projected a lot of confidence in him. Someone close to the King heard it and the word got to King Saul. Therefore, King Saul sent for him with immediate effect.

As David reported, he greeted the king and said, "Your Royal Majesty sir," worry not, I, your servant, David, will take down the Philistine empty vessel boaster. But the King responded, you cannot fight this Philistine, you're too young, and he has been a warrior from his youth.

David decided to submit his resume verbally to the king. He narrated to the king how he protected his sheep from being eating by a lion and another time from the mouth of a bear. He did not only rescue the sheep from their mouth, but he also killed them both. In addition, David proclaimed that, "the Lord who rescued me from the paw of the lion and the paw of the bear will rescue me from the hands of this Philistine." As a result, the king knowing there was no other choice anyhow, agreed to David's bravery quest. He dressed David with his own warrior attires, "a tunic, a coat of armor and a bronze helmet on his head." David took the sword and fasting it on the tunic. As he tried to walk, he couldn't move, so he requested all the warrior attires be taken off him; for he was not used to them.

What did David do? He took his shepherd staff in his hand, selected five smooth stones from the streams, put them in his pouch, his shepherd bag and with his sling in his hand, proceeded to the battlefield to fight the giant.

Chapter 2: Know your heritage and possess it

As David moved into the battlefield, the Philistine giant and his shield bearer started coming closer to David. As Goliath looked over from the mountain where they were, he saw a very young handsome boy glowing, for David was a very handsome charming young man. With amazement of his youthfulness, he said to David, "Am I a dog, that you come at me with sticks?" He cursed David out in the name of his gods. He invited David to come closer, so he'd give his flesh to the birds and the wild beasts.

Therefore, David responded with all boldness saying, "You come against me with sword and spear and javelin, but I come against you in the name of the Lord Almighty, the God of the armies of Israel, whom you have defiled." This day the Lord will deliver you into my hands, and I'll strike you down and cut off your head," David continued with his threat to the Philistine that he would give the giant's body and the Philistine army to the birds and beasts of the field. By this, he said, "the whole world would know there is God in Israel." And David continued, all eye witness that have gathered here today will know that "it is not by sword or spear that the Lord saves; for the battle is the Lord's and he will give all of you into our hands." After Goliath heard all David said, he became very spiteful and started marching majestically towards

David to attack him; David quickly ran towards the battle line to meet him. He reached into his bag and took out a stone, he slung it and the stone struck Goliath on the forehead. As the stone lodged into his forehead, he fell on the ground facedown.

David, bravely with confidence killed Goliath, the Philistine giant with a sling and a stone. David ran to where he fell, took Goliath's sword and cut off his head; which he took with him to present to King Saul, for evidence of his victory.

David was a mighty man of valor. This was confirmed by a song composed by their women as they celebrated victory upon victory of their battles led by David.

They danced and sang:
"Saul has slain his thousands, and David his tens of thousands."

LESSON: Watch your thoughts, how you position yourself in your mind, is what you will become. Also, watch your tongue on how you declare, there is power and authority in your words. Use your Identity to your advantage. David was confident because he knew whom he belonged to, the son of the Most High God.

CHAPTER THREE

Why God Shields Your Identity

As mentioned previously, God shields your True Identity, so others would not see the specific seed He planted in you, and to make sure the seed matures in order to produce good fruits to feed the people He brings your way. If the enemy discovers the type of seed inside you, he'd plot on how to prevent you from blooming and blossoming; so, you cannot produce any fruits. The enemy would send his agents to distract you, and to prevent your seed from been watered. And this we know, any seed planted in the ground without water, will perish; it will not survive.

Also, God will protect your seed to nurture to a healthy tree that will produce good fruits and will mature and ripe for the fulness of its sweetness.

The reaction to the extraordinary:

When your extraordinary ability comes out in the open, it will draw all kinds of attention, both positive and negative. Some will say, you're not qualified for such ability, in other words, they feel your maker has made a mistake, because you've gone above and beyond their expectations of you. While the one who is already up there says, you must not be allowed to grow to be a big tree like him or bigger than him; so

Chapter 3: Why God shields your identity

that you will not draw the crowd away from him/her. He forgets to realize there are so many humans in the world that need shades of more trees; and more fruits to eat.

Subsequently, the one very close to you, whom you share and confide in, says: why must it be him/her.? What has she got that I haven't got? For no justifiable reason, your success brings misery to them. Yet, there is a small crowd in the corner cheering, go-on, go-on, go-on; you can do it. When you feel you can no longer move forward because you're exhausted; when you look at their faces while they are cheering, you will draw strength from them. At this point you'll realize you can't give up, you must not quit because you're doing it for them. God assigned you to represent them.

The seed God planted in you is not for you; rather, is for you to grow it and bring fruits you will use to feed others.

Now, going back to the story of David and Goliath, the giant. When David saw the need of fighting the giant who was feared by his people; he was discouraged.

He was told that he was not qualified; too young and inexperienced. But, when he achieved victory, some citizens were happy because they knew he did it for them. And so, did David. Some questioned his achievement, why him? Outwardly everyone was relieved, the giant was gone, but in their hearts, not everyone celebrated David's subsequent victories.

When David left for the battlefield to fight the giant, King Saul inquired of David's identity. And Abner the commander of the army responded, "Your Majesty" I have no idea. And the King requested that he finds out who David's father was.

As David returned from killing Goliath, the army commander took him to King Saul, with the head of the giant in his hand, the king asked, "whose son are you, young man?" David answered, "I am the son of your servant Jesse of Bethlehem."

When you achieve beyond people's expectation, even those that know you, get disoriented; they get confused between who they think you are, and the true you whom they're looking at. This is because, their perception of who you are, is contrary to whom you really are. The amazement of your achievement paralyzes their speech, and they become dumbfounded in awe of your Real-Self-expressions.

Chapter 3: Why God shields your identity

David's Shielded Identity

David's story is a good example of shielded identity. In the previous chapter, in first Samuel, before David and Goliath's story, we were told that David played a harp for King Saul for a while.

After the Spirit of God left Saul, according to 1st Samuel 16: 14, God sent an evil spirit to torment him. For this reason, it was arranged, and he sent word to Jesse to send him his boy that keeps the sheep in the field. Each time the demonic spirit entered him, David would play his harp until the evil spirit departs from him. David was serving him, floating between playing music for the king and caring for the flock in the field.

Now, if David worked for him earlier, how is it that he did not know who David was when he went to battlefield and killed Goliath?

Due to the conception of limitation, King Saul's brain could not connect the little boy that plays harp for him, and the young brave mighty warrior in the battlefield. The conception of limitation in his brain refused to connect or merge the two identities because the rule of thumb says it's impossible. Can you relate to this?

Have you ever experienced something similar, where people undervalue your capacity or worth? When you achieve a greater success beyond their expectations, instead of praise, they'd malign you out of despise, and jealousy.

Although David received several awards from King Saul due to his successes, and he grew in rank in the army. But it wasn't long before King Saul became very fearful and envious of his achievements, so, he hated him even to death.

To reiterate the subject of knowing the real you, your true identity, the following principles are necessary:

- Incline to know and understand the real you from your maker's point of view.

- Do not settle for less by accepting the world's definition of you; the world does not define you for you do not belong in it, nor can any human see what is inside of you.

- Focus on the assignment given to you by your maker; wave off the environmental ambience, for the enemy is readily available to distract and attack.

- Everyone has a destiny. But the location, and the decoration of your destiny, depends on how and what you do with your assigned mission given you to fulfil on planet earth. The perception of other people in the world has no bearing on the outcome of the result of your destiny at the end of the rope; because you and only you can influence your destiny.

- Our creator made everything good for us. He mapped out a clear road on our journey to our destination. However, it is absolutely our decision to follow the existing plan or deviate from it.

How do you know and understand the Real You?

First, you must maintain a relationship with your maker; so, instead of listening to the enemy who doesn't want your progress and success, you will have the one who cares for you, your Lord, and friend. He knows what is good for you because all His plans for you are good.

Second, your maker knows everything about you, He knows your destiny, and therefore, He will prepare and guide you on how and where to better serve your purpose. All He requires is for you to be obedient. Cooperate with your creator.

Moreover, do not disregard your true self, the real you. Confidence comes by knowing who and whose you are. David had the confidence that he could take down the giant because he knew his true identity, and he knew that the Lord was on his side. His true identity is that he was a chosen child of the Most High God, an anointed of God and a man after God's own heart. And that was the revelation of his identity that magnet both friends and enemies into his life. David's "Coat of Many Colors," were his multiple talents and blessings from God. He carried a crown of favor.

PART TWO

Life Reflections

What is Your Why of Life?

Born Again to a Living Hope 1 Peter 1: 3-9 ESV

[3] Blessed be the God and Father of our Lord Jesus Christ! According to his great mercy, he has caused us to be born again to a living hope through the resurrection of Jesus Christ from the dead,
[4] to an inheritance that is imperishable, undefiled, and unfading, kept in heaven for you,
[5] who by God's power are being guarded through faith for a salvation ready to be revealed in the last time.
[6] In this you rejoice, though now for a little while, if necessary, you have been grieved by various trials,
[7] so that the tested genuineness of your faith--more precious than gold that perishes though it is tested by fire--may be found to result in praise and glory and honor at the revelation of Jesus Christ.
[8] Though you have not seen him, you love him. Though you do not now see him, you believe in him and rejoice with joy that is inexpressible and filled with glory,
[9] obtaining the outcome of your faith, the salvation of your souls.

Who Am I?

Who am I?
That the Sovereign God sent His only begotten Son to Earth,
to take my place and be crucified on the cross of Calvary.
Who Am I?
That Jesus, the Christ, paid with His blood so I might live eternally.
Who am I?
That my Lord left His heavenly glory,
came to Earth to redeem me so I can be saved.
Who Am I?
That there was a hallelujah in heaven
at the announcement of my conception.
Who Am I?
That saints of God rejoiced at my arrival on Earth.
Who am I?
That both the angels of heaven and the saints of God celebrated my rebirth.
Who am I?
That the Almighty God gave me a special name in glory.
Who am I?
That my Father, the Almighty God,

should send me out into the world,
to bring His lost children home.
Who am I?
That He endows His mercy upon me.
Who Am I?
That He sent His Holy Spirit to dwell in my heart.
Who am I?
The King of kings, the Lord of Lords,
Knows who I am.

I am, the precious daughter of the Most-High God.
I am, the apple of His eyes.
He knew me before I was conceived in my mother's womb
I am, the daughter of Zion.
I am, the precious one in the palm of the Most-High God;
So, no devil can snatch me away from Him.
He ordained, fortified me, and gave me a new name in glory.

I am, a chosen one, by the Most-High God.
No weapon fashioned against me shall prosper.
Jehovah Jireh, the El Shaddai, is my Father.
God the Son, Jesus the Christ, is my Redeemer,
Advocate, Savior, my King, and my friend.
In gratitude, what shall I say unto my Lord?

All I need to say is, thank you, Lord.

I invite you today to celebrate with me, the Lord's goodness.
His mercies are new every morning;
And His mercy endures forever.
Come, join me to experience the love of my Heavenly Father
What He has done for me, He will do for you also.
Though our needs may differ, I tell you the truth today,
Whatever your situation may be,
My Father will meet you at the point of your need.
He shall supply all your needs;

For His treasure is abundance.
He has a surplus of wealth.
For all that call Him Abba Father,
He brightens their hearts with everlasting joy.
Come, let us glorify and give praise to our Jehovah.
He alone we must adore,
He alone deserves our praise;
And in His name, we must worship.
Oh, give thanks to our Lord of Lords,
for His goodness endures forever.
We await His return,
To take us to our eternal home.
Hallelujah, we shall sing with the angels of heaven.
Hallelujah! Hallelujah!! Amen, and amen.

CHAPTER FOUR

The Quest of Life

In order to be accountable for your life, you must understand what life means to you. I want to start with some steering questions about life as it affects you, because from my observation, the meaning of life is different from one individual to another, depending on who you ask. And to some people, they do not know how to answer the question, "what does life mean to you?" If you are in this group, it's okay, you're not alone. Furthermore, some people thought they knew the meaning of life until they are hit by an unforgettable storm, and their canoe capsizes into the deep ocean; then they wonder, what is this life all about? Yet, to some, their answer is, "life is not fair". Okay! If you are in the category of life is not fair, why not start by knowing and understanding what life really is before you put a grade in your evaluation of life.

Here, we are going to do a little exercise, so we can move forward. This book is an experiential learning, a practice-based approach to learning. Our educational campus is the World, our discipline is LIFE, our subject is Human, and our topic today is "The Quest of Life". Now, take a notebook and a pen and answer the following questions:

Chapter 4: The quest of life

- Why do you do whatever it is that you do?
- What is your goal in life, and why?
- How do you know when you have achieved your aim?
- You have gotten that which you spent all your energy and time pursuing; now what?

Some people define life from the answers to the above questions. If you have answered the questions honestly, now, answer this question:

- What does life mean to you?

I have been opportune to ask some individuals these and/or similar questions at different time and settings, both professionals and students, in a seminar, individually, and in a classroom setting. What I discovered is that a lot of people focus on the pursuit of success as defined by the world's standard. Based on the individuals' answers, I see that humans have created four driving forces in life. These identified driving forces are the reasons human beings keep on pursuing and pushing themselves to attain something called success. The driving forces which people have identified specifically or indirectly are Identity, Purpose, Acceptance or recognition, and Security. They call these their drivers of life. But in reality, if your life's focus is on success, the way the world defines it, the above listed essential elements of life cannot be your drivers; rather they are what I call influencers of the driver of life.

In a later chapter, I'll share with you what prompted me to look into this topic, how it all started. Before I progress into the main theme of this book, I want to share with you why I'm writing this book.

Why Am I Writing This Book?

This book, *Discover Your Coat of Many Colors*, is written to inspire, motivate, encourage you, and to help you discover how to attract true success in life. It will help reveal the secret things of life, which were only secret because you never understood how to utilize them to your advantage yet. And, how to position yourself to prosper in every area of life, to redeem God's promises and to unwrap your divine blessings.

I am writing this book to remind you how important and precious you are to your creator. I am writing to remind you that everything you need in life is within your reach, it's already been made available, hence, success is within you. However, how you choose, your choice determines your end result. I invite you to take this journey of discovery with me to discover the true meaning of life, and what really drive humans in the journey of life. I am writing, so you don't have to spend decades of wandering and searching for the true meaning of life, because you need to start living the life which you were created to live.

In my many years of experiences and observations, intellectually and spiritually, I have come to understand that the quest of life is truly, all about freedom. It does not matter your class or the level of your success; whether you're rich or poor, depending on how you see yourself. Success does not necessarily mean abundance of money nor does poverty necessarily mean lack of money, as the world defines it. Our society teaches us that to be successful is to acquire a lot of money and be famous. Of course, having money is a good thing, however, it does not guarantee you freedom. True success is "The Everlasting Freedom" which is already available to you, but you are not utilizing it due to lack of spiritual knowledge. Is the thought of money controlling you, or are you controlling the way you think about money? If you are not sure, answer the following questions:

- Do you spend sleepless nights worrying or thinking about money?

- Do you ever worry that you won't have enough money to sustain you for the rest of your life?
- You have plenty of money, but do you worry what will happen to your money after you're gone?
- Do you love your money more than human beings?
- Are you constantly chasing money?
- Do you spend a lot of time thinking about money?
- Does having money give you a lot of concern about your security/safety?
- Are you living a fulfilling life because of your money?
- Does having money bring full joy into your life?

You got the drill? There are more questions you can ask yourself about your relationship with money, and what success really is to you. Having a lot of money does not guarantee you freedom, as it is defined spiritually.

Money is not evil. However, money is one of the major aspects of life that our enemy, the devil uses against us. Hence, the need for us to discover true success that will bring fulfilment, peace and joy into our lives.

Ride on with me to discovering the true success, in the journey of life and finding your destiny.

Chapter 4: The quest of life

Life, What is it?

In my quest of knowing the meaning of life, I sought the help of wisdom, and wisdom said the following to me:

Go to the middle of the universe, stand silently, and listen to the echo of the world; so, I did. As I listened, I heard two distinguished voices.

From the distorted heart, or the wallowed suppressed voice, I heard:

Life is hopeless, full of disappointments, and heartache,
Life is worries, doubt, fear, and anxiety.
Life is depressing, hateful, ugly, wickedness, and unfair.
Life is imperfect, full of brokenness, weeping, agony, and crying.
Life is natural, disasters, and destruction
Life is begging, chasing and hunting.
Life is learning, filled with illusions, unorganized and emotional.
Life is approval, seeking, heart beat and music.
Life is a journey, filled with drama and uncertainty.

Then, from the blissful heart I heard:

Life is hopeful, believing, and trusting.
Life is good, full of assurance.
Life is gracious, love, cherish, and happiness.
Life is beautiful, lively, and blissful.
Life is living, spiritual, and inward.
Life is sacrifice, giving, encouraging, and receiving.
Life is application, testing, and result.
Life is reality, certainty, and melody.
Life is a destination, supernatural, and eternal.

At the end of my observation, I went back to wisdom to share my findings. Surprisingly, wisdom helped me to realize that all I've listed above are not the meaning of life; rather, they are the expressions of life. Therefore, I asked wisdom to help me discover the meaning of life. And then, he sent me back to the Universe, but this time, I'm to go to the foundation of the earth, there that I'd find the creator's map and follow the path to the infinity. Again, I followed wisdom's instructions. As I went straight to the foundation, just like he said, I found an instructional manual with the map of infinity zone. So, I picked up the instructional manual and I began to study. Inside it, I discovered, you and I have a Holy God; our creator, God is a Trinity. I found out that we are created in His image, according to His likeness. Then He put us in charge of all His beautiful creatures on earth. He blessed us to multiply and commanded us to rule and take control over the earth.

The Human Makeover

"In the beginning, God created the heavens and the earth." God created this world and everything in it, both the visible and the invisible. After He created all His creatures, in the waters, on land, in the sky the firmament, and they were very good; then, He looked around and realized, all these beautiful things He created need a creature that will maintain them; in other words, He needed a manager, and a Leader. Been that He's full of wisdom, on the sixth day, He said, "let us create man in our image." He used plural because God, is 'Trinity', three in one: God the Father, God the Son, and God the Holy Spirit. Three in one, for there's no division in the God head. He has three personalities with three major functions at the same time.

Now, on the sixth day, the last day, He worked before He rested on the Sabbath day that He hallowed and blessed for holiness. He took some wet dirt from the earth and formed man. When He finished designing the physical man – the temple, to make him to be just like Him, He breathe through his nostril and transferred the spirit man He had created in His own image, into the molded house for man, and man became a living soul. To paint a clearer picture, God is a Spirit, He's not physical, therefore, we cannot see Him in the natural. But we know from His own word that man looks like God because, He said, "Let us make man in our image, according to our likeness;" {Genesis 1:26}. In the beginning, man was a spirit being that lives inside a body. And when the spirit man inhibited the body, the temple, a soul was formed, where God imparted His intelligence, creative ability, power, and authority, to take dominion over the earth and to manage and maintain all God's creations.

Unfortunately, after the fall of man, after man was deceived by the enemy, the devil, man lost his immortal inheritance and his composition changed. God sent Adam and Eve out of the garden of Eden because of disobedience, for "the wages of sin is death." The composition of their being changed, the flesh became dominant over the spirit man, because of sin. God gave man a will, freedom to choose. He did not create a puppet, He wanted man to be able to make decisions on his own, whether is good or bad. This reflects the degree of His love and care and trust for mankind. Besides been a caretaker for all God's creations, God created man for companionship, man fellowshipped with God in the garden of Eden until the fall.

God Redeemed Mankind

After the fall, the state of man became hopeless. God in His infinite mercy could not watch His children perish so, He rescued mankind by sending His Beloved Son to the world to take away the sins of mankind through "Death and Resurrection". The freedom of choice is still available to human beings. It is a fact that Jesus Christ died for all men, but the decision of salvation belongs to individuals because the human destination has doubled, and it's no longer one destination according to the original plan. According to the word of God, whoever repents and re ceives salvation, shall inherit eternal life. But whoever refuses to repent, shall inherit the damnation of hell fire reserved for the dragon, Satan and his followers.

What is Repentance?

Repentance is the acceptance of the Lord Jesus Christ; which means, you believe He's the beloved Son of God, who became the son of man, and a man of sorrow. He died for your sins, so you can be saved.

He resurrected and has gone to heaven, and He will come again. His second coming will be to take the saints to heaven. And after the destruction of the present earth, there will appear a new heaven and a new earth, according to Revelation 22, the restoration of Eden. And He will establish His Kingdom in this world and shall rule over His people through eternity.

Why not now?

Repentance alone does not guarantee you salvation. After repentance, you must be born again, through the baptism of water and the Holy Spirit. The water baptism is the submerging of your body inside water and raising it up. This signifies death, burial and resurrection. In other words, you died of your sins, buried, and resurrected with Christ. Then after the baptism of water, you'll also receive the baptism of the Holy Spirit, the Spirit of God. And you become a new creation.

The first human experience of the Holy Ghost was during the Pentecost, where Christ told His disciples to wait for the comforter before He ascended to heaven. The Holy Spirit is the third person of the Trinity God, whom Christ sent after He departed this earth. The Holy Spirit is to guide us into all truth. He is God living inside of us, those that are saved through Christ. The Holy Spirit is to empower us with clear understanding of the holy word, to continue with the work of Jesus Christ in the plan of God to redeem His children for salvation, before the end of the age. The indwelling of the Holy Spirit is for all who receive the salvation of our Lord Jesus Christ, the grace of God, by faith.

God, who knows the heart, showed that he accepted them by giving the Holy Spirit to them, just as he did to us. 9 He did not discriminate between us and them, for he purified their hearts by faith. Acts 15: 8,9. NIV.

Salvation is for all mankind, Jews and Gentiles, for Jesus Christ, the Redeemer, and Savior, came to the world, died and resurrected, that none should perish. However, the decision is personal, because God has given us the freedom of choice. Will you receive this available freedom and be out of bondage? Do not procrastinate, tomorrow may be too late. Why not now?

What Really Drives You in Life?

Previously, we learnt according to the world's standard that four essential elements are identified by humans

as life drivers. These are identity, purpose, acceptance, or recognition, and security. And I said, based on the world's focus, the items mentioned above, I consider them life influencers, because the world's focus, the center of attraction in life, based on the world's standard is SUCCESS. Therefore, success is the human driver in life. As a result of this theory, I define success this way:
Success is a direct result of the energized force from the life influencers of humanity.

What is the True Meaning of Life, and Success?

As I stated earlier, the representation of the essential elements of life known as the human drivers in life is often misconstrued. In this book, we will dissect each of those components of life and their functionality, as we study the steps on the journey of life and destiny.

In a nutshell, LIFE is the air of freedom. The process of life is all about preparation. Therefore, Success is freedom. **So, what is freedom?** Freedom is when the real you can see beyond the illusions of the cosmic world, to recognize your heritage, and decide to stand on your original foundation. In other words, freedom is the ability to recreate your own world within this evil world, and to utilize the knowledge given to you by your creator. It is also applying His divine wisdom to identify and claim all that is yours, and you have dominion over them because it is your heritage. Your creator, your maker, your Heavenly Father, made this provision for you right in the beginning. You and I are not supposed to live a life of want and lack because we have. Our Father made that provision. **As He is, so we ought to be.**

In reality, the four essential elements that human beings define as life drivers: Identity, Purpose, Acceptance, and Security, cannot be life drivers because they are part and parcel of the human's life. They are the components or essential elements of life. **They are key factors to the essence of human existence on planet Earth.** As human beings, when you struggle with the identification of your identity—knowing who you are, and when you look at success as a driver in your life, you will see that your identity and your purpose intertwine. For you to know your purpose, your mission in life, you must first identify who you are, the real you. You cannot discover your real purpose in life with a misguided identity. A misguided identity is who you think you are, based on other people's perception of you. Other's perception of you does not reveal the true you, as they cannot physically see the real you inside. Your body is only a house where the real you lives.

The world by error had built the human life drivers around success. While in reality, all human is chasing is "freedom". The devil has led many astray, thinking they are still in bondage. Hence, they live their lives struggling to reclaim freedom, which was lost in the garden of Eden, by our foreparents, when the devil deceived them. We need not struggle to reclaim that freedom any longer because our Father sent us a Redeemer about two thousand years ago. As a result, we were granted victory, freedom, power, and authority. Therefore, all that was given to us at creation, the foundation, is rightfully ours. Our creator commanded us to take dominion over all His creatures. Whosoever receives His gift of grace is a new creation, is entitled to the Father's heritage, as we are heirs with His beloved Son, our Savior. When you recognize who you are, your true identity, you have freedom, and freedom is success, which is within us. When you have Jesus, the Christ, by receiving the grace of God, you have life; for Jesus is life.

It can be confusing sometimes, knowing the purpose of your existence on planet Earth. Everyone wants to be valued and recognized as an individual. Hence, when people seem invisible in the eyes of others within their environment, they feel like outcasts, or unimportant. The feeling of not belonging can result in low self esteem which will affect their confidence. In some cases, it can lead to depression. In other words, people strive to be accepted wherever they belong. Lastly, on the four essential elements of life, is security. Security is a very vital aspect of life. There are two types of security in our everyday living—safety and wealth, which is financial security. Looking outwardly for the above needs will lead to dissatisfaction and disappointment.

This book makes known the awareness that you cannot achieve the above essential elements of life by looking sideways; meaning you can't get them from any man. You can only receive all by looking up for freedom, which is received through the recognition and acceptance of the gift of the grace of our Lord Jesus, who came to reclaim for us what was rightfully ours. In the first place, you must know your identity, a child of the Most High God.

In summary, if there is any driving force in human life, it is freedom. Freedom is not something you acquire, it's something you receive. The offer is been made waiting for your response. Freedom is free, it is the grace of God. Receive, claim it, and you shall live a blissful life.

All mentioned above will help you to be accountable for your life. Moreover, freedom comes by understanding the principles of life.

PART THREE

Battling With The Feeling Of Inadequacy

The young Prophet Jeremiah wrote:

The LORD gave me this message:

"I knew you before I formed you in your mother's womb.

Before you were born I set you apart and appointed you as my prophet to the nations."

"O Sovereign LORD," I said, "I can't speak for you! I'm too young!"

The LORD replied, "Don't say, 'I'm too young,' for you must go wherever I send you and say whatever I tell you.

And don't be afraid of the people, for I will be with you and will protect you.
I, the LORD, have spoken!"
Then the LORD reached out and touched my mouth and said,
"Look, I have put my words in your mouth!
Today I appoint you to stand up against nations and kingdoms.
Some you must uproot and tear down, destroy and overthrow.
Others you must build up and plant."
Jeremiah 1: 4-10. NLT

CHAPTER FIVE

Are you afraid of your call?

Conquer fear by trusting God.

When you see yourself from the eyes of your creator, doubt and fear will have no room, and you shall live victoriously. Confess the Lord Jesus as your Savior, remain faithful and obedient to His word, then "ask the Father anything in His name," He said, and you shall receive. Prayer is the key to eliminate doubt and fear. *I sought the Lord, and He heard me, And delivered me from all my fears. Psalm 34:4 NKJV.*

God set Jeremiah apart as His prophet to proclaim and enlighten God's people in the ways and precepts of God; to be His mouthpiece to his generation. Our God is still speaking today through the prophets of today and His chosen men and women representing the everlasting Kingdom of God, with the everlasting message of eternity. Listen to them so you can discover all about you and this life; they will lead you to the right path. Start now, right here. By the time you read this book to the end, you'll know your true identity, who you are; you'll know how to identify your mission on earth, and what path to follow that will guarantee your arrival at the right destination. Search the scriptures for divine wisdom, ask the Holy Spirit to give you understanding in your quest of knowing the true meaning of life as you seek knowledge from His living word.

Chapter 5: Are you afraid of your call?

Your life was already planned out before your arrival on earth. You were born for a mission, to be significant, distinguished in every aspect of life, and to prosper beyond measure. Discover your real identity, and become all God wants you to be. It's high time you reclaimed what the enemy stole from you. Our Lord and King fought the battle for you so, you'll live a blissful life. Why then are you still mopping, feeling sorry for yourself? If you lacked awareness, now you know, you have been freed two thousand years ago. All your Creator made available for you is for your taken, so use it to support the harvest of His vineyard. Know this, you were born for such a time like this.

Perhaps, you are one of His chosen Ambassadors, and His mouthpiece in this world. Then, boldly go to the vanguard of His vineyard, as He has sent you. Do not be afraid; don't allow the world to disqualify you, for the world does not know what you carry. Your creator qualified you before you were formed in your mother's womb. Go out and mirror Jesus, bringing hope to the destitute, the over worked and undervalued workers of the great harvest. Don't concern yourself with what to say or do, the God Almighty will also touch your mouth as He touched Jeremiah's.

For I know the thoughts that I think toward you, says the Lord, thoughts of peace and not of evil, to give you a future and a hope.
Then you will call upon Me and go and pray to Me, and I will listen to you. Jeremiah 29:11,12

What Can I Do?
That which you do to serve others, is your ministry

Jeremiah is not alone. Sometimes we struggle with our mission in this world, what God wants us to do to accomplish His purpose through us. Do you fall into this category? If this is you, it's alright, you're not alone. God will never leave you to work it out alone either.

Every child of God is uniquely created by God, the Creator. We were all made in God's own image; yet, every one of us is individually created, meaning we have no duplicates. In the whole world, there's only one you. And there is a specific assignment given to you to fulfil. If you neglect your assignment without accomplishing it, know that such an assignment will be left undone. Before you were born, like Jeremiah, God gave you a special assignment, then fortified you with some gifts {talents} to help you accomplish the assignment for His purpose. These gifts grow out of a seed of greatness, the seed of life, that God, the creator planted inside of you. The seed is a ministry to be nurtured and developed. Then He lights a candle and put in your hand as he sends you out to the world, so the world will know you have come with a mission.

God will not send you out to the world if He had not equipped you. What He said to Jeremiah applies to all His children. Before your egg was fertilized in your mother's womb, He knew you because He created you, and equipped you with all necessary software applications suitable for the hardware of your body that He has formed or created, to better serve the specific assignment or purpose He wants you to fulfil.

After equipping you before you were born, as He sends you out into the world, knowing the evil that dominates this world, He provides you with a guaranteed security. Security of protection against the evil forces of this world. And he prospers you in your ministry, whatever you're to do, financially and in health. Moreover, your Creator makes a promise to you, to go boldly without fear because He'll always be there for you and with you; to teach you, lead you, protect you, and provide for you. What a guaranteed promise from the one who knows you best; He knows all your weaknesses and your strengths. If God the Almighty trusts you that much, why are you limiting yourself? Why not believe Him and trust Him by believing in yourself, by accepting what He says about you without doubt. See yourself from the eyes of your creator and be victorious.

Why Do You Struggle For Human Acceptance, While God Is Your Cheerleader?

God knows what He put inside of you, so He encourages you, "you can do it my child, you are able, you're wonderfully made, if you don't do it, nobody else can. I'm holding you in the palm of my hand, trust me and move. Go get my children out of the world. Encourage those in the field to persevere in the harvesting of the crops." "I will always be with you." "He who is in you, is greater than he who is in the world." No more excuses. It doesn't matter how the world sees you or what they say about you. What God says overrides every negative thoughts and propaganda of the enemy and his agents. Be obedient and honor God by serving your purpose on earth. You serve God by serving mankind.

That which you do to serve others, is your ministry.

Know the real you, accept yourself, and be in love with yourself for there's none other like you in the whole world. When you understand you, the "real self", your heart will be joyful, you'll be bold and confident. Then others will see the reflection of your inner self on the outside, and they will see you from God's viewpoint and will accept you and love you as well. In other words, what you project outside from your inward being, is what will come back to you. However, this does not mean the whole world will accept you. You will always have enemies for different reasons. Sometimes for just being alive, people will hate you. But remember, God's got you covered. You're untouchable. "No weapon fashioned against you shall prosper;" declares the Lord of Host.

All you need to do is believe His word, be obedient, trust and stand on His promises. Then ask Him to order your steps, and He shall direct your path.

Order my Steps Lord!

Order my steps, Lord;
You are the only one I want to listen to.
The world is full of discouragement, anguish, and pain.

But I am convinced that You are on my side.
Help me Lord, not to depart from Your presence.
An ordered step, I request from You.

O God when You speak to me,
Turn the volume up so I can hear You.
When You speak,
put conviction in my heart to know You are the one.
Give me the understanding to know what You say to me.
Then lead the way, so I can follow.

Sometimes I hear a still voice in my heart,
I wondered, is it You Lord, speaking to me?
Or is it just my heart wondering on facts of life?
Dear Lord, speak to me, and
Let me recognize Your voice.
So, there'll be no doubt in my heart,
You're leading my way.

Whom Do I Belong To?

Genesis 1:26 to 28, as stated previously, clearly declares to whom you belong to, and your heritage. The God who created you, with lots of love in His heart, mapped out a master plan for your life. So, you will live a blissful life. A life filled with hope and

Chapter 5: Are you afraid of your call?

purpose, with guaranteed peace, love and happiness. Then the devil, full of hate for you, got jealous and said, not on his life. He would not watch you enjoy while he suffers. As a result, he came up with an evil plan to make sure he deprives you of your birth right. The devil came to you in disguise as if he genuinely loves you; told you all sorts of lie, and you believed him out of ignorance.

Therefore, you lost all hope, because you feel there's no way out; you're doomed. Guess What? There's always a way out with God. While God was putting together His master plan for your life, He knew the evil one is on earth roaming aimlessly, He foresaw the enemies evil plan against you; hence, God provided a solution beforehand.

The sin of disobedience that humans, You and I committed deserved a death penalty. However, instead of us taking that punishment Satan caused us, our loving Father, our creator, sent His only begotten Son to earth to take up a human identity, to die in our place. This is how the devil our enemy was defeated. God could not allow His son and daughter, you and I to perish. He said, they are the apple of my eyes. They are my beloved children. I'll cleanse and sanctify them; wherever they go, my presence will be with them, I'll give them the desires of their hearts, and I'll prosper them. And He said to the devil, go to hell; I will always love my children. I'll draw them to myself, they will be my people and I will be their God.

God has given you eternal freedom with guaranteed promises; why are you still in bondage? I'm writing you today to wake you up from your sleep, to remind you, who you are, and whose you are. To remind you of our Lord's goodness and to reveal to you the master plan of God. Even when you trip or fall, you'll see His hand stretched out to lift you up.

For I know the plans I have for you," declares the LORD, "plans to prosper you and not to harm you, plans to give you hope and a future. Jeremiah 1:11 NIV
For God so loved the world that He gave His only begotten Son, that whoever believes in Him should not perish but have everlasting life.

For God did not send His Son into the world to condemn the world, but that the world through Him might be saved. John 3: 16,17. NKJV.

Receive the amazing grace of our Father God;

and from Jesus Christ, the faithful witness, the firstborn from the dead, and the ruler over the kings of the earth.

To Him who [a]loved us and washed us from our sins in His own blood, and has made us [b]kings and priests to His God and Father, to Him be glory and dominion forever and ever. Amen. Revelations 1: 56 NKJV

Then all the saints of God gathered together in celebration of our Lord's goodness.

And they sang a new song, saying:
"You are worthy to take the scroll,
And to open its seals;
For You were slain,
And have redeemed us to God by Your blood
Out of every tribe and tongue and people and nation,
And have made [a]us kings[b] and priests to our God;
And [c]we shall reign on the earth." Amen.
Revelation 5: 9,10. NKJV.

If you are a King/Queen and/or a priest by Jehovah, no one can curse you nor cast a spell on you for the Lord has fortified you with kingly and priestly anointing. Eccl 10:20. Do not allow yourself to be deceived again by Satan, the liar. Use your faith against every challenge. The word of God says: "whoever trusts in the Lord shall not be put to shame." Do not be intimidated by anyone, not even by the devil himself. Open no door for the evil one; "fear not," for the Almighty God, your creator, is always with you. He will stand by you, and He has equipped you for every battle that comes your way. He will protect you. The Lord has given you the best weapon to fight the enemy, the sword and spear, the holy word, to be used with the name above all names, Jesus Christ; "at the mention of His name, every knee shall bow."

In David and Goliath's story, it was the name of the Lord that David used to defeat and killed Goliath; it was not the stone. If it were the stone, he would have falling backward, according to the law of gravity, but by him using the authority of the name of the Lord, the giant, the enemy of children of God, had to bow, falling forward and gave up to the ghost. Our Abba Father is loving, gracious, and merciful. Yet, 'Mighty and Sovereign'. He fights for and takes care of His own. All you need do is believe, have faith and trust Him. Remember, He knew you before you were conceived in your mother's womb. His thoughts of you are all good and never evil. The Almighty God holds you in His palm, where no evil can touch you nor snatch you away from His presence. The scripture says:

> But the eyes of the LORD are on those who fear him,
> on those whose hope is in his unfailing love,
> *19 to deliver them from death*
> *and keep them alive in famine.*
> *20 We wait in hope for the LORD;*
> *he is our help and our shield.*
> *21 In him our hearts rejoice,*
> *for we trust in his holy name.*
> *22 May your unfailing love be with us, LORD,*
> *even as we put our hope in you. Psalm 33: 18-22. NIV.*

Praise God! Our God is marvelous indeed. He speaks in a clear and simple language, for easy understanding. His Love and Assurance is for sure. So, what is your excuse now?

In His Presence

"Deliver me O Lord, from my enemies;"
For you are my refuge.
"Teach me to do Your will,
For You are my God;"
In your presence, I find peace and joy.
Uphold me in your righteous palm,
to completely depend upon You for direction.
Then show me your way, the true path to everlasting life.

And grow in me the confidence of depending on your goodness
without doubt and fear;
so, your will shall be fulfilled in my life. Amen.
—*Inspired by Psalm 143:9,10*

When you faithfully surrender all to God, your burdens, troubles, heartache, and every pain the enemy dishes out, God will surely manifest His presence. You cannot fight the battles on your own, therefore, leave everything in the hands of God through prayer, and He will take you to where you ought to be.

When you pray, be bold in your request, and pray in faith.

Now, Lord, look on their threats, and grant to Your servants that with all boldness they may speak Your word, by stretching out Your hand to heal, and that signs and wonders may be done through the name of Your Holy Servant Jesus."

And when they had prayed, the place where they were assembled together was shaken; and they were all filled with the Holy Spirit, and they spoke the word of God with boldness. Acts 4: 29-31; NKJV.

This is an unmerited mercy our Father God has given us—the indwelling of the Holy Spirit. But we must willingly accept its functions in our lives to always direct our paths and thoughts. Romans 8: 8-11, tells us that anyone who does not have the Spirit of Christ, does not belong to God.

PART FOUR

Destiny Awaits!

⁸ So then, those who are in the flesh cannot please God.
⁹ But you are not in the flesh but in the Spirit, if indeed the Spirit of God dwells in you. Now if anyone does not have the Spirit of Christ, he is not His.
¹⁰ And if Christ is in you, the body is dead because of sin, but the Spirit is life because of righteousness.
¹¹ But if the Spirit of Him who raised Jesus from the dead dwells in you, He who raised Christ from the dead will also give life to your mortal bodies through His Spirit who dwells in you. NKJV.
- Romans 8: 8-11. NKJV

CHAPTER SIX

Why Am I Here?

I mentioned earlier that every human is born with a special seed-gift inside of him/her. The seed needs to be nurtured and developed to be able to serve its purpose, which is to aid in accomplishing your mission of being on earth. This means that every individual has a God-given purpose, assignment to accomplish on this planet which can only be assumed or completed by that person.

How do you determine what your purpose is?

First, let's imagine the seed God deposited in you as a regular seed that the farmer plants on the ground, when it germinates, it shoots out the planted old seed and it takes the roots to the ground. As it grows into a tree, it produces different components such as the stem, branches, leaves, flowers, fruits, and of course, the roots. Every component of a tree has a specific function. Likewise, the seed inside of us germinates and grows into a tree that has different components called gifts or talents. Remember, not all trees grow flowers and/or fruits. But every tree has roots to hold it firm, some branches and leaves. The fullness of a tree differs from one to another. Sometimes it depends on the ground, and sometimes it depends on how the plant is nurtured. The components of the tree from the seed planted inside you by God are called gifts or talents, which are to be developed and used to achieve your God-given purpose. To answer the question of determining your purpose, you must be aware of the specific gifts your seed has produced.

Your gifts will lead you to your purpose. However, if you're still not certain, to identify your gifts, think of things you love doing, things you do that others go wow! and you know you're good at it. Gifts are your intellectual abilities, and/or your mental capabilities, used for creativity that results in a physical form. I define it this way because they cannot be seen, they are hidden inside until they are expressed in the physical. For example, a soccer player is not known to be good until he exhibits his talent in the open. Also, a fashion designer, until his work is seen outwardly, those around him including himself, will not know his capabilities. Furthermore, there are other gifts, when expressed out, they cannot be seen but experienced or observed by others. In other words, the expression of human gifts produces tangible or intangible results. Example of a tangible result is the case of a designer. You can physically see his drawings and finished clothing. But for a gift like leadership ability, there's nothing physical to see. You can only experience or observe a leader's ability; its measure is strictly by quantifying his communication skills and actions. And how his influence affect those around him.

Can you have more than one talent/gift?

The answer is yes, absolutely. I believe every human being is born with multiple talents, however, not every talent even when developed have equal value, meaning you can be good in all, but not all will give you satisfaction.

The gifts or talents that will lead you to your purpose in life must have the following criteria:

- Your ability must be outstandingly noticeable by others.
- You must be very passionate about doing what you do.
- It must give you peace and satisfaction.
- Your love for what you do must supersede your need for the financial benefit.
- Your inner peace and joy for doing what you do must be felt by those around you.

I mentioned previously, that your gifts are given to you to serve others. We serve God by serving other human beings. This is to say that serving our purpose on earth entails serving our fellow mankind. We cannot accomplish our purpose in the absence of other human beings. Yet our purpose is designed to satisfy or fulfil God's purpose on earth through us.

It is very vital to pay attention to the calling of God because if you do not identify your call or mission early in life, you will waste a lot of time chasing the wrong dream[s], moving in circle without making a head way; until you arrive at your God-given destiny before everything clicks.

Does it mean if you're doing an assignment which is the Will of God for you, you'll face no difficulties?

On the contrary, every mission comes with challenges, especially if it is a special assignment from God that will be for His glory. It will magnet great obstacles from the enemy because of the battle between good and evil. However, remember, God's promise to Jeremiah applies to you and me too. He said we should not be afraid, that He will protect us. And He will equip us for what He wants us to do. He touched Jeremiah's lips and put words in his mouth. He will not only send you out, but He will also give you all necessary to achieve what it is, He wants you to achieve for His glory.

Sometimes, to get to the real mission, you'll go through a process; and most of the time, a very difficult process. On the way to your destiny, you will experience some unpleasant situations that will discourage you from moving forward, but for His grace. To explain what I'm trying to say, I'll share with you a story of a young man who was sure of a bright future because not only did he have a solid family foundation, God's revelations to him in dreams and visions propelled him to believe such until the table turned for the worst.

Problems visited him in chains until his whole life became a nightmare, contrary to the revelations of God. Does this sound familiar to you? I know it does to me. It makes you wonder, knowing that God is not a human being that He should lie. At the same time, you cannot shake off the experiences you're going through because they are real. The situation makes no sense, and you are confused. What can you do? Well, let's see how the story of this young man unfolds.

CHAPTER SEVEN

Experiencing the Illogical

What Do You Do, When Your Experiences Are Contrary To Your Belief?

Once upon a time, was a young tenacious seventeen year old teenager, named Joseph. This young man had everything good; he was smart, handsome, intelligent, and wisdom beyond his age. However, his wisdom was not ordinary; he had special divine wisdom from God. Furthermore, he was a dreamer, and could also interpret dreams. His innocent character and attributes resulted in his naivetés in dealing with his household enemies.

Joseph came from a very large family. His father had him at his old age, he was the eleventh out of the twelve sons of Jacob. His aged father loved him so much, more than life itself. He was very close to his father. It was no secret that he was the favorite of his father among the sons; for his mother was the youngest of Jacob's wives whom he loved very dearly.

One day, Joseph returned from attending to the flocks, for they were shepherds. His father had a big business of rearing Cattles, Lambs, and Goats. Jacob trained and absorbed all his children into the family business, attending to the flocks was their means of survival. Now his father invited him into his suite and asked him to sit down. "Joseph my son," he said. "Yes, Papa," he responded. The father then continues, "you know I

Chapter 7: Experiencing the illogical

love you very much, and the Lord has favored you with wisdom. There's something about you that I don't see in any of your brothers. So, pay close attention to our family business and learn all there is to learn about it. And if you have any questions, you ask me. My intention is to enlighten you first, on the way of our Lord. Second, on the indepth of cattle raring, which is our way of life and then on other facts of life.

Joseph's father Jacob is also known as Israel, at the end of his talk with his favored son, he pulled out a robe, he made specially for him; in the scripture, it's described as "a coat of many colors" and he gave it to him. The coat was symbolic of Jacob's deep love for Joseph. It also reflects the trust and respect Jacob had for his son, Joseph. The coat also reflects the makeup of Joseph; what makes Joseph, Joseph. The Coat had many colors, vividly noticeable to the eyes of others, it attracts attention, pleasing to the eyes, and joy to the hearts that see it. The joy comes from the likeness of the colors on the special coat.

Unfortunately, the coat of many colors did not attract only the good, it equally attracted the bad and the ugly. The ten older brothers of Joseph knew the position of their little brother Joseph, in their father's heart, hence, they hated him with passion. To add salt into injury, Joseph now would be parading their sight with this special coat, a thought they could not bear. Their dislike of him increased; they had nothing good to say about him. They called him little spoilt brat. He was considered too pompous to their liking. This is because Joseph was loaded with knowledge and filled with divine wisdom. His intelligence made his brothers uncomfortable. His I. Q was way beyond his age and level.

And it came to pass, one night, while the silence of the whole compound sounded like a grave yard, the divine spirits of heaven visited Joseph, and revelation was given to him. When morning arrived, he woke up with the detailed memory of the revelation. He excitedly ran to his brothers to share the wonderful thing that had happened to him while asleep in his bed, the divine power visited him. Big brothers listen to this, you've got to hear this, he said excitedly. I had this amazing dream last night, we were all binding sheaves of grain out in the field, suddenly, my sheaf rose and stood upright, while your sheaves gathered around mine and bowed down to it. This young naïve boy had no clue what he had just done; he created life enemies, that were not pleased with him in the first place. He could not comprehend that even though they were blood brothers, the brothers were never on

Chapter 7: Experiencing the illogical

the same boat with him. Anything good happening to Joseph was poison to their hearts.

After sharing his dream with his brothers, they exploded saying, "do you intend to reign over us? Will you actually rule us?" Their dislike of him was intensified, and their hatred of him escalated.

Joseph, with the mind of a child still never learned his lesson from the previous encounter with his brothers. Again, a few days later, he had another dream, yet this time as before, he went to his brothers announcing his divine encounter while asleep. "My dear brothers, I just have to tell you this: I had another dream, and this time the sun and the moon and eleven stars were bowing down to me." This time, when he shared his dream, his father was also present. The dream sounded so ridiculous that even his father, Jacob, was ticked off; so, he reproached Joseph saying, what type of dream is that? "Will your mother and I and your brothers actually come and bow down to the ground before you?"

The brothers were happy at their father's reprimand of Joseph, their little brother. They felt they had more ammunition now to discredit him and his intellectual wisdom. Little did they know his wisdom was beyond intelligence, rather he was divinely gifted, therefore, they could not obliterate it, nor its recognition.

Despite the father's reproach, Jacob, their father took cognizance of the supernatural favors of his son Joseph. However, he wanted Joseph to be humbled and wised up to acknowledge that the deep things of divine nature, cannot be discussed loosely and casually. Even their father knew, his older sons never liked Joseph, and they hated him with passion. However, it never occurred to him that that hatred would lead to a desperate act of removing his beloved favorite son completely from the stage.

One day, in view of the responsibility Jacob bestowed upon Joseph about the family business, he called Joseph and told him he was going to send him out on an errand. Joseph listened to him attentively. Their home city was called Hebron, and their cattle farm was at Shechem. So, he said, I want you to go to the farm at Shechem to check on your brothers and the flocks, how they are faring. Then come back to report to me the situation of things down there. Yes sir, I'll go at once to do as you have requested, replied Joseph.

The Beginning of Joseph's Nightmare

Joseph set out on a journey to Shechem to see about his brothers and the flocks as his father requested. Unfortunately, by the time he arrived at Shechem, his brothers and the flocks had relocated to Dothan, as he was informed by a strange man. He decided to trace them down there, and he found them near Dothan.

As soon as his brothers sited him from afar, one of them said to the others, "here comes the dreamer!" He has come to see what we are doing, to supervise us. And they said, "let's kill him and throw him in one of the dry wells here in the field, and let see what will come of his dreams." When Reuben, the most senior of them all heard this, he was troubled, he did not welcome the idea at all. He tried to trick his other brothers to just throw him inside a well and not to shade his blood. He wanted them to throw Joseph into the well and not kill him, so he could rescue him and send him back to his father.

Therefore, when Joseph approached the field where they were, they stripped him of his beautiful coat and threw him inside the dry well. When they gathered to have their meal, they looked up and saw a caravan of Ishmaelites from Gilead approaching. The people carried all kinds of spices, balm, and myrrh, heading to the market in Egypt. Judah suggested to his brothers, "look my brothers, by killing Joseph, we gain nothing; after all he's our flesh and blood brother. Instead of killing him, why don't we sell him to these traders; at least we will get something from them." And all present agreed. So, they sold Joseph to the Midianite Merchants; they pulled him out of the well and gave him to his new owners. By the time Reuben returned so he could rescue Joseph, he investigated the well, the boy was no longer there. He got angry and tore his clothes, wondering what he would say to his father.

The brothers took Joseph's robe, slaughtered a goat and soaked the ornate robe inside goat blood. As they got home, they handed the coat to their father asking him to examine it if it was his son Joseph's coat. Jacob admitted it was Joseph's coat and concluded some dangerous wild beast had devoured him. He immediately tore his clothes, put on a sack cloth and he mourned for Joseph, his beloved son; and no one could console him from weeping.

When the Midianite Merchants got to Egypt, they sold Joseph to Potiphar, King Pharaoh's captain of the guard. There, Joseph was thrown in into the hard labor camp with other slaves.

Joseph could not comprehend what was happening to him. It made no sense to him whatsoever. He kept on asking himself these questions: "what have I done to deserve this type of suffering? What did my brothers tell my father? What will happen to my old father, and my little brother, Benjamin? What if they will do the same to him?" There were no answers to his questions.

Joseph Under Potiphar

Potiphar was Joseph's Egyptian Master. While Joseph was serving as a slave in Potiphar's house, the Lord prospered him with favor. When his master saw that the Lord was with him because everything Joseph touched prospered, he became very intrigued by him. Hence, he promoted him to his personal assistant; he put him in charge of everything in his household. Joseph became his manager for all his welfares both at home and in the field. And the Lord blessed everything Potiphar owned because of Joseph.

The angel of darkness again came to destroy the good thing in Joseph's life. Joseph, been a very handsome and well-built young man, his presence radiated and magnet his master's wife. One fateful day, the wife of Potiphar invited him to sleep with her; but he refused.

She tried to drag him in, pulling on his shirt, instead, Joseph removed himself from the shirt and let her have it; so, he ran away from that house.

What did Mrs. Potiphar do? She screamed very loud, and the guards assembled in her court to see what was wrong! She lied to them that the young man her husband put in charge of their household wanted to rape her, hence she screamed, and he dashed out in a hurry. The guards hearing her accusation wondered amiss. Potiphar raged with anger when the report got to him; therefore, he threw Joseph back into the prison. He sent him to the same cell as to where the king's prisoners were confined. Yet, in the prison cell there, the Lord was still with him; for God's favor followed him wherever he found himself. This is because God loved him, and Joseph was very devoted to God, and he loved God also.

And it came to pass that the king's two prisoners had dreams the same night, but, did not know the meaning. Joseph, with his caring nature, when he came to attend to them in the morning noticed their sad countenance on their faces, he demanded to know why? Both the Chief Baker and the Chief Cup bearer had a dream in the night, but didn't know the meaning, so they were troubled. They shared their dreams with Joseph. As the Lord's hand was upon Joseph, he interpreted their dreams accurately. After giving a favorable interpretation of the dream to the cupbearer, Joseph requested a favor from him. He told the cupbearer that after the King restores him to his former position, he should put some good words to the King on his behalf, to get him out that prison. He even shared with him the dilemma of his exit from his Hebrew land, and the innocence of his slavery and prison life. Unfortunately, when the Chief cupbearer was out because the King had restored him back to his position, he completely forgot about Joseph. Joseph spent another two hopeless years in that prison, until the voice of destiny was heard.

CHAPTER EIGHT

The Voice of Destiny

No one can override the plan of the Almighty God; the voice of destiny must be heard.

At the end of two more years in prison, thirteen years in all that Joseph was in incarceration. From the day he was forcefully taken from freedom till that day was thirteen years. Joseph, an innocent soul, wasted in the prisons for no just cause. It made no sense. And he could not explain it, nor did he understand why? Yet, he never wavered in faith, trusting God.

One day, King Pharaoh gathered the great magicians and the wise men of the land together. The King addressed them and said, "I have gathered you all here today for a very good reason. Last night, I had a dream, the first dream came in my night vision, at the end I woke up. I slept again, and a second dream came and at the end of it, I woke up again. But I do not know what they mean. For this reason, I've gathered all of you, the great intellectual men and magicians of my province to interpret the dreams for me. The King told them the details of his dreams. There was no one who could understand the dreams to interpret them.

Suddenly, the Chief cupbearer remembered the young man who interpreted his own dream about two years ago, and the late Chief Baker's dream, when they were in prison together.

My King, he said. I just remembered a young Hebrew boy who interpreted our dreams, myself and the late

Chief Baker. He further told him the accuracy of Joseph's interpretations.

The King ordered for Joseph to be brought to his presence immediately; as a result, Joseph was prepared to meet the King. He was washed up, dressed in a nice apparel to look presentable to meet with the King. Upon his arrival, Pharaoh said to Joseph, I had some dreams which no one could interpret, but it came to my knowledge that you can interpret dreams. Joseph replied, "I cannot do it, but God will give Pharaoh the answer he desires." (Pharaoh's dream, Genesis 41: 17-25).

Then Joseph answered and said, "my King, both your dreams mean the same thing. The Sovereign and the Almighty God had revealed to you what He intends to do for the next fourteen years. In a nutshell, he told the King there would be seven years of abundance of food, and seven years of famine. The famine would be so severe that the soil would crack, and crops would have no moisture to grow. Many would die of starvation. Moreover, the agony of the scarcity of food would cause people to forget all about the seven years of plenty. The suffering would be so much that they would not remember the good times.

King Pharaoh was greatly troubled by this revelation, so he expressed his thought loud by posing this question, "what can we do?"

Therefore, Joseph, in his divine wisdom, advised as follows: "My King, this is what you need to do, look for a discerning and wise man, put him in charge of the land of Egypt. Appoint Commissioners over the land to take a fifth of the harvest of Egypt during the seven years of abundance to store up under Pharaoh's authority. These reserves are to be used during the years of famine to avoid the disaster of starvation."

The plan sounded amazing to the King and his cabinet members. Then, Pharaoh asked, where can we find such a man, a God-fearing man, filled with the Spirit of God? Instantly, Pharaoh realized, there's no better candidate for the job than Joseph himself. And Pharaoh ordained Joseph, his commander in chief, to oversee all the welfare of Egypt. Joseph was crowned the governor, to oversee every affair of Egypt from then onward, second in command to the King. And the King removed his signet ring from his finger and placed it on Joseph's finger. He dressed him in robes of fine linen, he put a gold chain around his neck and gave him a chariot to ride on. After establishing his status, the King said to him, as from today, you shall

Chapter 8: The voice of destiny

be called Zaphenath-Paneah. Furthermore, he gave him a wife; Asenath, daughter of Potiphera, the priest of On. Currently, Joseph was thirty years old.

The favor of God followed Joseph and he prospered in everything he touched. And because of him, Egypt prospered beyond measure during the seven years of abundance; they could no longer take count of their grains and food stuff in the store house due to bountiful harvest, which were reserved in the cities all over Egypt. King Pharaoh and his people respected Joseph and loved him greatly.

Starvation in The Land

When the seven years of abundance had passed, famine started invading the land of Egypt and the surrounding nations. After sometimes, the famine was becoming unbearable in Canaan, Joseph's homeland; as such, his father Jacob gathered his sons together and said, my beloved, we cannot continue like this else we perish from starvation. I heard that there's grain in Egypt, make hast and go down there to purchase food items for us.

The ten brothers of Joseph embarked on the grain hunting journey to Egypt. When they arrived in Egypt, they proceeded straight to where the Governor of Egypt was distributing grains to purchasers. And they bowed to the governor. As soon as the governor sited them, he knew they were his brothers, but he pretended like he didn't know them and spoke unkindly to them as if he was a stranger, for his brothers no longer recognize him as Joseph. Of course, they could not even suspect their brother to be up there, for it is not comprehensible. It wasn't just logical to the human mind. Guess what? At this very moment that they bowed to the governor of Egypt, their brother Joseph remembered the dream when he was a teenager. And that very moment was a fulfilment of that dream.

Then Joseph who was called Zaphenath-Paneah accused them of being spies. And they said, "No my lord, your servants are no spies." They called him lord, and themselves, servants. In the process of proving their innocence, they told their family story about how many they were, the youngest of their brothers with their aged father, and one was no more, which was referring to Joseph.

Regardless of their explanations, Joseph was adamant about the accusation of them being spies against Egypt, and he put them to test to clear their names

Chapter 8: The voice of destiny

or prove their innocence. He declared, "as long as Pharaoh lives you will not live this place unless your youngest brother comes here." He asked that one of them should go and get their little brother, while the rest of them would be locked up in the prison cell. The governor's demand did not soothe well with these brothers, as a result, they were all locked up.

On the third day, Joseph called the brothers and said, I am a man who loves God and wishes to do right by him. I will give you the benefit of doubt to prove your innocence. One of you will remain here while the rest of you will go and take the grains to your starving family. When you come back, you must come along with your little brother so that I'll know you're been truthful. However, if you ignore my request, then, you will not see my face if you come.

The brothers discussed among themselves saying, they were receiving a pay back from God for the evil they did to Joseph. Reuben even had a moment of I told you so to his brothers, for he warned them when they were plotting evil against Joseph about two decades ago. As they were talking among themselves, Joseph was hearing what they were saying, and his heart was broken all over, and he wept. He moved away from there to compose himself before returning to the scene. He had Simeon taken from them in handcuffs, in their presence and the other nine were let go. Joseph ordered that the money each paid for their grains be put back in the mouth of their sacks without their knowledge.

When they got home without Simeon, they sat their father down and explained their experiences in Egypt and the demand of the governor. Their father Jacob reprimanded them for revealing they had another brother at home. He was not about releasing Benjamin, the only child remaining of Rachel, his beloved. He took a firm decision about not letting Benjamin travel out of his sight. He was afraid if anything happens to his boy, that would put him fifty feet under the soil.

The Brothers' Return to Egypt

After they had consumed all the grains brought from Egypt, Jacob saw the need of sending his boys out to Egypt again to buy more food for the family. His sons reminded him of what the governor told them, that they would not see his face if they didn't come with Benjamin. Besides, their brother Simeon is still a prisoner in their jail cell. They made it clear to their father, they would not dare show their faces there by themselves, else they could be seized too.
Hence, Jacob had no other choice but to succumb to their request, and he released Benjamin to accompany

Chapter 8: The voice of destiny

them. Then he asked them to put together some products of the land and package them as a gift for the governor. He said, "take the best of honey, a little balm, some spices, myrrh, almonds, and pistachio nuts." Also, he gave them double the amount they needed, one for the previous purchase they found in their sacks, the other half for what they'd buy. He prayed for them and they departed for Egypt.

Upon their arrival in Egypt, they proceeded straight to Joseph, the governor's steward to explain about their silver coins found in their individual sacks. They told him they didn't know who put them there. However, they brought it back and they came with more silver weights to buy more. The steward told them not to be afraid and reassured them he got their payment. He added, perhaps the God of their father decided to release some treasure for them. Then, Simeon was brought out to join them. And the steward took them to the governor's house; where they were given water to wash their feet in preparation to meet with the governor and to join him for lunch as they were told.

About noon, the governor, Joseph came back home, and they presented their gifts to him. They had some interactions and had lunch.

The Silver Cup Setup

When it was time for the brothers to head back to their nation, Joseph instructed his steward to give them as much food as they could carry. Also, that they should put in the mouth of their sacks of grain the money they paid for the grain in each of their sack. In addition, he instructed the steward to put both his silver cup and his special silver dish in the bag that belongs to the youngest of the brothers, and so he did.

At day break, when they set out to return to their nation, before they could get out of the city, Joseph sent his steward after them and instructed him on what to say. When the steward caught up with them, he repeated the words his master instructed him to say to the brothers: "why have you repaid good for evil? Isn't this the cup my master drinks from and uses for divination? This is a wicked thing you have done." And the sacks were torn, and the items were found in their little brother Benjamin's sack.

They were all astonished because they knew the boy was not a rogue. They wept and tore their clothes, and all returned to the city. When they got to Joseph, the governor's house, they fell on the ground pleading for mercy, for the governor to pardon them. Joseph said to them, what is this you have done? Don't you

Chapter 8: The voice of destiny

know that a man like me can find things out by divination?" Judah replied to him, "what can we say?" He questioned how they could prove their innocence, as a result, he offered the governor to enslave them including the culprit, who had done the wrong. And Joseph responded, God forbid, that I should do such a thing! He demanded that only he who stole shall become his slave. And requested the rest of them to go back peacefully.

The brothers were stunned and speechless for a moment, then Judah summed up courage, went closer to the governor to plead. He rehearsed to the governor how they told him they had a little brother who was with their aged father. And if the boy should leave home, their father would die. Never the less, you insisted he must come, else, we won't see your face. Judah further offered up himself to be the lord's slave in exchange for his little brother, saying, he won't be able to look at their father's face if the boy doesn't return to him.

Hearing all Judah said, Joseph lost his composure and wept loudly, that both the Egyptians and people in the King's palace heard him. So, he sent away all his attendants to go out of the scene, and he revealed his identity to his brothers; and he asked, "is my father still living? His brothers couldn't answer because they were astonished and terrified, standing right there in his presence. They thought that was an opportunity for Joseph to retaliate for the evil they did to him. Instead, Joseph asked them to come closer to him and he embraced them. There was weeping and joy, crying and laughter at the same time. They could not believe their ears and their eyes.

Furthermore, Joseph asked them to forgive themselves, that the situation was divinely orchestrated. They were only there to fulfill the plan of God. It was the Will of God that he had to come to Egypt first in preparation to what they were then experiencing, to reserve their lineage; and all that belong to them. In addition, he requested them to go and bring his father to Egypt, with their entire family. He promised to take care of them by giving them a piece of land in Goshen, where they could rare their Cattles and live in abundance despite the famine. When word reached Pharaoh, he and his household were pleased that Joseph's brothers were in town. Joseph's brothers were sent back home with lots of food, and they were given a carriage which was to be used to convey their father down to Egypt. Joseph further admonished his brothers not to quarrel on the way back to Canaan.

Upon their arrival in Canaan, they shared the good news to their father Jacob. He was stunned hearing the unbelievable news, and he didn't believe them. After much explanation, telling him his son oversaw

Egypt, and they detailed him of their predicament, which was orchestrated by their brother Joseph himself. And seeing all that Joseph sent with them, he accepted they would pack and move to the land of Egypt; and so, they did.

On their way to Egypt, they stopped at Beersheba, to offer sacrifices to the God of his father Isaac. In a night vision, God spoke to Jacob saying: "I am God, the God of your father. Do not be afraid to go down to Egypt, I will go with you to Egypt, and I will make you a great nation there. I will surely bring you back again." Go in peace for Joseph's own hand will close your eyes himself, said the Lord.

When they arrived in Egypt, there was great joy, a great reunion celebration. So, Joseph established his father and their entire family in Goshen. And they lived happily ever after.

A Reflection of Joseph's Story
Romans 8: 28-31 NKJV

And we know that all things work together for good to those who love God, to those who are the called according to His purpose.

For whom He foreknew, He also predestined to be

conformed to the image of His Son, that He might be the firstborn among many brethren. Moreover whom He predestined, these He also called; whom He called, these He also justified; and whom He justified, these He also glorified. What then shall we say to these things? If God is for us, who can be against us?

What type of storms of life are you facing today? It does not matter the depth, and the height of it; it doesn't matter how frightening it may seem, know that God is working it out for your own good. Jesus is in the midst of your storms, holding you. Even when it seems like you cannot feel God's presence, still believe, and trust Him, standing on His promises to you and me. All you need to know is how much God loves you, and let the grace of our Lord be enough for you. If the God Almighty is on your side, who then can be against you? Our Redeemer lives; this is your assurance. Stand on the promises of God. His word will never go void.

The Glory of God Comes Down
Acknowledge the Lord Always!

Psalm 105 NKJV
1 Oh, give thanks to the Lord! Call upon His name; Make known His deeds among the peoples!

Chapter 8: The voice of destiny

2 Sing to Him, sing psalms to Him; Talk of all His wondrous works!
3 Glory in His holy name; Let the hearts of those rejoice who seek the Lord!
4 Seek the Lord and His strength; Seek His face evermore!
5 Remember His marvelous works which He has done, His wonders, and the judgments of His mouth,
6 O seed of Abraham His servant, You children of Jacob, His chosen ones!
7 He is the Lord our God; His judgments are in all the earth.
8 He remembers His covenant forever, The word which He commanded, for a thousand generations,
9 The covenant which He made with Abraham, And His oath to Isaac,
10 And confirmed it to Jacob for a statute, To Israel as an everlasting covenant,
11 Saying, "To you I will give the land of Canaan As the allotment of your inheritance,"
12 When they were few in number, Indeed very few, and strangers in it.
13 When they went from one nation to another, From one kingdom to another people,
14 He permitted no one to do them wrong; Yes, He rebuked kings for their sakes,
15 Saying, "Do not touch My anointed ones, And do My prophets no harm."

16 Moreover He called for a famine in the land; He destroyed all the provision of bread.
17 He sent a man before them Joseph who was sold as a slave.
18 They hurt his feet with fetters, He was laid in irons.
19 Until the time that his word came to pass, The word of the Lord tested him.
20 The king sent and released him, The ruler of the people let him go free.
21 He made him lord of his house, And ruler of all his possessions,
22 To bind his princes at his pleasure, And teach his elders wisdom.
23 Israel also came into Egypt, And Jacob dwelt in the land of Ham.
24 He increased His people greatly, And made them stronger than their enemies.

What Are the Lessons Learned From Joseph's Story

There are six key lessons we learnt from Joseph, and I'll briefly discuss each of them.
- OBEDIENCE: From the story, we learned that Joseph was an obedient child. He was obedient to his father; he listened and obeyed the word of his father, Jacob. It was his obedience that took him to the field to check on his brothers and the flocks per his father's instructions.

Chapter 8: The voice of destiny

With disregard to the fact that Joseph was wrongfully enslaved, he remained obedient to God. He did not waver in faith. He maintained his relationship with God, carried on with the principles his father bestowed upon him, to honor God, and trust in the Lord. He kept the faith.

- **PERSEVERANCE:** Joseph persevered in spite of his illogical circumstance. Although Joseph had no justifiable reasons as to why he was in captivity. He knew his brothers sold him out of pure wickedness on their part. However, Joseph's belief system tells him God had allowed the whole event to come to play for a very good reason, even though he did not know what. He kept to the belief that God loved him. He refused for his circumstance to cause him to react negatively. He did not curse God, nor his brothers, who put him there, nor his masters. He was in total obedience and everything he touched, God prospered. In all the stages of his dilemma, Joseph persevered.

QUESTION: Imagine yourself in a similar situation as Joseph, what would you do?

- **SELF CONTROL:** Joseph, a young handsome

and vibrant man who had been denied of the good life pleasure was given an opportunity to have it all; yet, he restrained himself. Some young fellows today would have chosen the pleasure by pretending to be obedient to his master, while disobeying and disrespecting, by sleeping with his wife. Had he failed the test, he would have jeopardized his relationship with God; therefore, depriving himself and his entire family of God's grace and blessings.

This story has taught us that having selfcontrol will help us maintain and retain our status with God. Secondly, we know that in every test, whether from God or the enemy, it is always the devil that carries out the temptations. Therefore, it is absolutely important to live in the presence of God always, so that God's presence in you and around you will not only repel the devil but will guarantee you victory always. In addition, having selfcontrol helps you to persevere in an uncomfortable situation because you know that God always has the final answers if you believe.

- TEMPERANCE: One thing that fascinates me so much is Joseph's temperament. He remained calm the whole time; even when Potiphar's wife accused him falsely, and his master threw him into the prison cell without a hearing. Yet, Joseph was not bitter. When he went to render some service to the chief Baker and the Chief cup bearer, he forgot about his own situation, he inquired of them, what was troubling them. Not only did he show concern for them, but he also listened and helped solved their problems. What a selfless act of kindness. He was renounced for his meekness.

QUESTION: If you were Joseph, would you have cared for anybody else? Or, would you have said, "is none of my business; who is listening to me?"

- SOBERNESS: Joseph's sobriety is enviable. In the whole Bible characters, the only character in the Holy Scriptures that reminds me of Jesus, the anointed one, is Joseph.

In fact, when you think of his soberness, I lack adequate words to describe him. So, I consulted Merriam Webster; and these are words that explain what I mean by soberness, according to Mrs. Webster:

The word sober in the contest of this story means: commonsense, commonsensible, commonsensical, firm, good, hard, informed, just, justified, level headed, logical, rational, reasonable, reasoned, sensible, solid, valid, and wellfounded. Wow!

What other words come to mind when you think of Joseph? Write to complete the following up to ten words. Lovely. Witty, ingenious, vivacious, caring, outstanding, eminence, preponderance, _____,_____.

QUESTION: How does each of the above words describe Joseph? Answer with a reference point in the story.

- FORGIVENESS: Joseph forgave his brothers, not 99% but 100%. He forgave them completely. Not only did he forgive them, but he also admonished them to forgive themselves, and not blame each other, nor quarrel among themselves.

He embraced them, welcomed them back to his life with an open heart. Amazing!

Joseph understood that God allowed the devil to use them that way, so his family would not perish during the great seven years of famine. The all-knowing, God, always knows the plan and the ways of the devil in advance; so, He always provides a way of escape to His children. He never abandons His own. Let His grace be sufficient for you; and you'll always be victorious, no matter what.

My brothers, sisters and friends, under the umbrella of the Trinity God, and to all reading this book, let forgiveness be embedded in your character. Do not hate, live forgivably always, as the scripture teaches. This, you cannot do on your own, unless you let Jesus in, in your heart. Allow yourself to mirror His image, and let His righteousness glow out of you.

May the peace of God, the joy from the fountains of His love, marinate your heart to live a blessed and a joyfilled life, that His name alone shall be glorified.

In the Midst of Storms

Remember that I have commanded you to be determined and confident! Do not be afraid or discouraged, for I, the Lord your God, am with you wherever you go." Joshua 1:9 GNT

When the storms of life are raging, hold on to the 'Rock of Ages'. He is your hope and your security. The holy word of God is your defense and your weapon.

When the enemy is pointing an arrow towards you, or plotting any kind of evil against you, fence yourself, your family, and anything that concerns you with these words: 2 Chronicles 20: 15-22.

As my Lord lives, I shall not be afraid nor be discouraged.

I will stand still, for this battle is not mine but the Lord's.

I stand firmly in faith, because I know my Father shall deliver me from all my troubles; my enemies shall be put to shame.

I shall live and not die, for my destiny awaits. What shall I render to my Lord? Gratitude, praise and worship; for His love endures forever.

I believe and trust in His covenant with me, that "no weapon fashioned against me shall prosper." For His anointing over me is my repellant and a covering shield over me, my family, and my generations to come. His angels encamp around me and all that concerns me twenty-four-seven. In Jesus Mighty Name, I stand on God's promises. Amen.

Let us hold fast the confession of our hope without wavering, for He who promised is faithful. Hebrews 10: 23 NKJV.

For God has not given us a spirit of fear, but of power and of love and of a sound mind. 2 Timothy 1:7 NKJV. Hallelujah!

PART FIVE

Demolish Evil Foundation & Build On The Rock

Building on a Solid Foundation

[24] *"Anyone who listens to my teaching and follows it is wise, like a person who builds a house on solid rock. [25] Though the rain comes in torrents and the floodwaters rise and the winds beat against that house, it won't collapse because it is built on bedrock. [26] But anyone who hears my teaching and doesn't obey it is foolish, like a person who builds a house on sand. [27] When the rains and floods come and the winds beat against that house, it will collapse with a mighty crash."*

Matthew 7:24-27 New Living Translation (NLT)

CHAPTER NINE

What is Your Foundation?

As I stated earlier, I'd share with you how my quest of knowing the meaning of life and the human drive(s) started. In about a decade ago, I was privileged to counsel some eleventh-grade high school students, on a one on one career conference. These students in a private school, in the previous year, had taken all the subjects required in senior secondary school or high school, both science and arts subjects.

Now, at the starting of eleventh-grade, they were required to select an area of concentration to prep them for college (university). I told the academic Dean and the Principal that I'd like to handle the career counselling of the students that year. My position as the head of schools, I didn't have to do that, but I thanked God I did afterwards. First, I requested for the students' previous performance record including their previous term promotion examination, to enable me to study their academic background. On the day of the conference, in a group, I gave them a screening test, a three-part question:

Part A: I asked them to list down their selected subjects and area of concentration. They had three choices, pure science, pure arts and the basic, which is somewhere in the middle, meaning, some science and some arts subjects. Part B: They were to indicate their future career choice. Part C: They were asked to explain why they made those choices.

I remember some students who wanted to be Medical Doctors, some type of Engineers, and Lawyers, only because they never had one before in their lineage, and they have to be the first or their parents want them to, or simply because they want to make a lot of money to become bread-winners for their families, and to some, simply for prestige. Yet there was a handful who selected those areas because is the best thing for them according to their academic strength, and interests.

As I continued reading, I discovered some students whom I expect them to choose the way the other students chose, those who would do well in those areas according to their academic strength and performances, but they didn't. Some of their selections shocked me; while some of them left part B and C blank. My human logic convinced me they were indecisive yet because they were not sure. However, I was a little puzzled by that, because based on the little time I had spent with them, I knew some of them were not the unsure or confused type. As a result, instead of conferencing with them that day, I converted it to an oral interview because I had to clarify those issues that were not making much sense to me.

During the oral interview, for the students who left part B and C blank, I discovered contrary to my assumption, they were not unsure at all. Rather, they were convinced they won't be forging ahead after secondary school. And when I asked why? Their answers were that they won't be going beyond high school because they have no one to sponsor them, or that their parents could not afford to send them to the University. At this point, I was glad I listened to that small voice known as instinct that told me to handle this process myself. I found out some students were about to drop out of school not only because their parents could not afford to send them to the University, but because they could no longer afford to continue in our school and could not even buy text books. Some, their grades dropped the previous year due to lack of text books. These students gave me a lot to chew and ponder on that day. For every one of them, divine wisdom gave me the right answer suitable for their situation.

For this group of students from impoverished homes, knowing that the main reason I chose to be in the educational ministry is to help students like them, even

Chapter 9: What is your foundation?

though we had many benefiting already, sometimes paying the staff salary was a continuous challenge. Regardless, I made sure those students finished their high school education without the fear of being sent home for school fees, and for some, the school also took care of their school fees and text books, just to give them that stepping stone. Despite my assurance to this group, one student told me not to waste that money, so I'd not be disappointed. This marveled me. For privacy reasons, I'll not include the details of my conversation with this young man, however, I asked him why he had chosen to come back to school that term. He said he missed his friends during the holiday, so he decided to come till when it's time for school fees drive then he'd not come back.

His situation was challenging to me, but thank God for His divine wisdom, a familiar story came to mind. I asked him, will you have an open mind to hear a true story? He said yes, so I started, "once upon a time, there was this young boy, at the end of his primary school, they took an entrance examination to enter secondary school. Being a very brilliant boy, he passed the exam with flying colors, it was a breeze for him. Then came the day of the interview, he performed excellently, according to his interviewer, until he was asked the final question, who his sponsor would be. This boy was very honest, he told the interviewer he had no sponsor, his parents could not afford to send him to secondary school. As a result, he was not assigned to any secondary school.

Later, there was war in the nation, which put everything to a halt. After the war, all children were asked to go back to school. Even though this young boy already graduated from primary school, they were all compelled to go back to elementary six. And at the end, due to his academic excellence, he was among those given scholarship by the then governor of our state to attend secondary school. In his secondary days, he continued with his academic excellence, in the end, he had an excellent performance. And for this reason, he was offered a scholarship to attend University, there are more into the story," I said to him. My point is this, don't limit God. I finished the story by letting him know, not only that the young man was giving scholarship to attend University, he studied abroad, in the United States of America.

This my student had a puzzled look on his face, then he said, Mommy, such stories only happen in fairy tales. So, I replied, "this is not a fairy tale, it's real. The young man is related to me. Your brother?" He asked. No, although my elder brother studied in the USA too and he is also a chemical engineer like this other man I'm talking about. "Do you mind if I ask who?" Not at all, I said. The man is my husband. He had a second chance because someone encouraged him to go back to attempt that which he thought was impossible. Our lives today is a direct result of that decision. Perhaps I won't be his wife today. That decision enhanced not just our immediate family, but our extended families too, I added. I closed by telling him whatever decision he makes today, will affect many lives in the future, some he doesn't know yet. In summary, this young man continued in our school, and then took his West African examinations a year later and passed with flying colors.

For the group of students who wanted to be medical Doctors, Engineers, and Lawyers, but had no academic excellence in their chosen area of concentration, whose reasons were: money, prestige, parents said so, or to be the first in their families. I did not tell them bluntly, look, you don't have a strong academic background in that area, nor did I tell them how ridiculous their reasons were. However, I gave every one of them something to think about, without deciding for them.

One of the students who wanted to be a medical doctor for the wrong reasons came smiling, all pumped up. Perhaps he was feeling so good about himself thinking I'd be so proud of him, wanting to be a medical doctor. I couldn't help but smile with him, it's just his nature, more like a clown. After he settled, I proceeded, so, you want to be a medical doctor? Yes Ma'am, he responded assuredly. "I want to make a difference in humanity, especially, I will be the first medical doctor in my family." "You can make a difference in humanity in many ways," In fact, in all we do, when we are obedient to the directives of God, in one way or the other, we're serving mankind, and this is how we serve God through people." I answered this way because the first part of his answer was to please me, he was just throwing my own words back at me.

I continued, "Medicine is a very good profession; it requires some patience, a lot of hours at work. Still, it's very rewarding I presume because you'll see the changes you make in human life, reviving their health. Instantly, I changed the conversation to indirectly draw his attention to his strength. I commended him on their previous term debate, how I enjoyed it. I'm so proud of you. I also loved the drama you directed, it comes so natural with you. You kids bring joy to my heart, keep it up. You are one of the role models here in this school for the junior ones. Again, I commended him on his eloquent speeches and his outspokenness during heart to heart, a program I created, a forum where students could express themselves freely, by

Chapter 9: What is your foundation?

letting the staff and management of the school know their concerns, and opinions on certain issues that concerned or affect them. At this point, he couldn't contain himself smiling and saying, thankyou Ma'am, thankyou Ma'am.

After the chatty chat, I came back to the business of the day, career planning. I told him the same thing I told his classmates: "You have the right foundation, and because of the foundation, I believe you will make the best decision that will lead you to your purpose in life." He had a blank look on his face and I knew he didn't get it. "Do you have a question?" I asked. "How do I know that purpose?" I replied, "the answer is within you." Now it was time for me to explain his foundation. First, thank God that He created a unique and distinguished you, and has equipped you with everything you need, the special talents to complement your physical you, to enable you face the world. Second, we thank your parents. They sent you here to receive a well-rounded education to solidify your foundation for the tasks ahead. And that's a huge sacrifice on their part because they want the best for you.

Here in this school, you have received a strong intellectual and spiritual foundation in the last four years. Using your intellectual and spiritual knowledge, you should be able to identify your strengths and weaknesses . You've been taught on how to strengthen and maintain your strengths. You've been taught on how to use your weaknesses to your advantage, and how to channel them to reverse to your strength.

"Spiritually, what have you learnt so far? Oh, I have learnt so much, especially since you came to be with us, you have taught us so much about God, and other things." "Give me some examples," I said.

You told us, the only limit is the ones we set for ourselves because we can go beyond the skies if we put our minds to it. So, I rephrased the question, "tell me what you have learned?"

You showed us to pray in all things. You said with God all things are possible. I had to make correction, so I interjected. Actually, I didn't say that, the Holy Bible says that. Then he rephrased, I mean we learnt from you that there is nothing God cannot do. I also learnt that when I ask God anything, I should ask in faith believing I receive it, and it will be done unto me." This student gave me about five answers before I stopped him. Then I said, "you have learned well. Now, is time to put them in practice.

Chapter 9: What is your foundation?

I continued, our career guidance conference is in two weeks. Before then, as you go home, first, go to God in prayer, ask Him to direct your path. Tell Him you do not understand your purpose here on earth, let Him help you to know what it is and to understand it. This is an opportunity for you to put in practice what you just told me. Go and put your faith to test. After speaking to Him, be silent for some moments so you can hear His answer when He speaks." He had that concerned look on his face again. So, I added, you've been taught how to hear God, right? He smiled and said, "yeah, that's right!

Also, you have two weeks to cogitate and assess your decision. In addition, for the next two weeks, you'll have another opportunity to study all the subjects like you did last year, one week is the normal revision of what you studied last academic year, and the second week you'll have the intro lectures on those subjects at your current level. Pay attention to every detail, and I guarantee you, with God's guidance, you'll know exactly what you need to do, and what will work for you. He thanked me, and when he was about to leave, I asked him, can we pray together? Yes Ma'am. And we prayed.

This student showcased a positive attitude on the outside when he arrived in the interview room.

Contrary to his outward projection, he had a battle inside because he knew the truth about himself. He came with the expectation of me to intervene in that battle. However, by the time he left, his attitude changed drastically. He was no longer empty inside, the inner battle was replaced with peace and certainty, even though he didn't know what the end result would be. The difference, now he has faith that convicted him to believe in a positive outcome, whatever that maybe. He left the scene with that assurance that brought him peace and joy to his heart. I didn't fight the battle for him, rather, I showed him hope.

A week later, this young man came back to me and said, "Ma, I changed my mind." Before he could say anything else, I stopped him. "Don't say anything else about that please, unless you have something else to talk about. Your career conference is in five days. Use this time judiciously in your analysis because you'll be making a major decision that will affect the rest of your life. Don't be in a hurry, if what you want to tell me today is still the same thing you want me to know, then, tell me at that time." He may have been a little disappointed, but I know he learnt another lesson from that experience, because **every moment brings us a new lesson, and there's always a lesson to be learned in every situation.**

Personally, I learned a lot on that precareer conference day.

The Career Conference

On the career conference days, each student was scheduled for fifteen minutes; I only averaged about six minutes per student. About 97% knew exactly what to do and where they should be. 2% only, needed a little contribution from me to guide their decision. 1%, I had to get their parents involved, not because they didn't know what to do. They were academically very sound, however, their parents wanted to live their lives through them. The parents wanted to correct or make right their own missteps in life, in the lives of their children. Instead of me counselling the students, I ended up counselling some parents.

In a nutshell, I had to explain to them, it was not possible for one to live his or her own life in another person because we are all individuals with different assignments on earth. If for some reason, you feel you missed your call, what God had asked you to do, if God wants that done, He will raise another Himself to do it, and you don't have a say in it. Also, I shared with them that our God is a God of second and more chances. I told one parent, "the bicycle laying on the side of the road, which she fell off of it either because of a hill or a valley, she can pick it up and hop on it again. This time the ride may be smoother because she'd gotten more experience and she is now more mature. This parent told me, it was too late to pursue her dream. So, I asked her, "did God tell you that? No!" she responded. I quoted her earlier statement; "you said you felt that that was what God wanted you to do." For whatever reason, you couldn't do that, "and now, you are not only compelling your daughter to do it for you, you want her to have regrets later too. If she agrees to live your dream, What happens to hers?"

Furthermore, if you feel, according to you, that God wanted you to do that, why are you not including Him in that decision now? What decision? She asked. I'm glad you asked, you're making two decisions for God without Him. First, you didn't want to do what He asked you to do because of the delay, you concluded it is too late. Secondly, you want to assign another person to do it for you without consulting Him, thereby encouraging her to neglect her life destiny. I'm sure that's not your intentions. She concord with me saying, she never looked at it that way. In addition, she admitted the whole thing was her fault, and that she would explain things to her husband.

As for the Medical Doctor young man, from the moment we greeted, and I asked him to have a sit,

Chapter 9: What is your foundation?

he started laughing. As I looked at him, I busted into laughter myself, without knowing why we were laughing. Within a moment, I composed myself, and he had no choice but to quit. "What was that all about?" I asked. He told me he was laughing at himself. "Why?" He replied, "I just can't imagine I did that. I'm not very good in chemistry, I hate dissecting anything including insects in biology, and especially, I can't stand the sight of blood." So, what made you pick medicine during the screening? He replied, "I was so confused with the voices in my head. The noise from the voices overshadowed the small voice that was coming from my heart." When he came to me, he thought I would tell him no, and also decide for him the obvious. If this had happened, he'd tell his parents I said no because he'd not do well. "have you made a decision now? Yes Ma'am. I want to study Law because I know I'll do well. I can practice as a Lawyer, work in the Government or in a big corporation. And more importantly, I want to be a politician, to be the voice of my people. Whether I become a Lawyer or a politician, I want to represent the voiceless of my society."

As he spoke, I saw a genuine honest determined young man. It was like a different person than the character I perceived of him as a clown. "What about the noises in your head?" His response, "from the first day I cried to God and poured my heart to Him, the noises stopped, both in my head and in my house. It was as if Jesus said, "peace be still"." What about the voice in your heart? I can hear it very clearly now; that's why I didn't want to wait the two weeks. Although I'm glad I waited because I had an opportunity a few days ago to sit my parents down and told them I couldn't handle medicine." "what was their reaction?" "Mommy, prayer works oh! They supported my decision. My dad only said, I shouldn't be like regular Lawyers, that Lawyers are liars. I should always stand for the truth." "That was a very good advice," I commented. The voices in his head were the voices of his loved ones.

Do you see how the whole situation played out, without God, and with God?

Then, on my side, you see the obvious benefit of relying on God's wisdom.

We are still talking about "the meaning of life, to you." I'll repeat the questions I asked at the beginning, in case you haven't answer them yet.

1. Why do you do whatever it is that you do? In other words, what motivates your quest of life?

Chapter 9: What is your foundation?

2. What are you trying to achieve, and why? If you look at the questions very well, you'll notice that the questions are one and the same. And if you have honestly answered the questions, you'd see that the answers are also the same.

We have discovered in the earlier chapters that what the world teaches us as our drivers of human life are based on illusions, they are not real. They are there, but not being utilized the way our creator designed them to be utilized because our wrong believes give us misguided information. The human mindset says, the devil is in control, hence, we still live as slaves. However, if you have the knowledge that through the cross of Calvary, the blood of Jesus paid the price for us and reclaimed our heritage, then you'd know that you are no longer a slave. You are a free daughter or son of the Almighty God, who assigned you to subdue and take dominion of everything He created. You are to run, manage your Father's business as His CEO. You have the power and authority to command and declare how things should appear or be in your world.

The power and authority to change your world is in your tongue. Declare to receive what your Creator already made available to you, and so shall it be.

The scripture says, "Ask, and it will be given to you; seek, and you will find; knock, and it will be opened to you." Whatever you desire, ask with faith believing you shall receive, in the name of our precious Lord and Savior Jesus Christ. It shall be done unto you.- Matt.7:7.NKJV.

Live in freedom, take what belongs to you; you're no longer a slave. However, remember your creator, our heavenly Father is still in control. Consult Him always and write your report to Him frequently. Worship Him always; praise, pray, and glorify Him, continually.

Lessons From The Career Conference

I cannot quantify my benefits from that career conference experience; the knowledge and wisdom I gained were insurmountable both in the natural and in the supernatural realms. Not only did I rediscover myself, but I was also affirmed through that experience. I discovered one of my main objectives for my mission on earth. And for this reason, I recommitted myself to helping people, especially the youth, to fully understand the true meaning of life; what life is all about, by helping them first to recognize and analyze their quest of life, and the importance of knowing

Chapter 9: What is your foundation?

their true identity. And to help them discover or rediscover the power in our thoughts and the power in our tongues.

Also, I helped the students to rewire their mental faculty supernaturally, in order to set apart reality from fantasy, which helped them to see a clearer picture to decisively make a more realistic decision that would be more beneficial and fruitful for them in the future. What happened at that conference helped build the students' confidence, giving them an opportunity to act and feel responsible for their own lives, hence, revealing to them that their opinion about themselves matters more than anybody else's. Your mindset controls everything around you. It is a "catalyst" for the life you're living.

Most importantly, the conference revealed the importance of laying your foundation in the right foundation, our Lord Jesus Christ, to yield good dividends. When you lay a child's foundation in God and build her on the rock, the enemy will not succeed in pulling down her foundation, no matter the storms and waves of life because her foundation will always stand the test of time. She will remain a victor.

Be accountable for your life by having your mindset right, for you to produce the right and proper fruits from the seed your creator planted in you. Be wise!

CHAPTER TEN

Understanding The Principles of Life

To understand the principles of life:

- You must have a clear understanding of your belief system.
- You must allow your faith to work for you; choose to live without fear and doubt.
- Your belief must supersede your logic, and it must program your mind to fly on trust zone.

Have A Clear Understanding of Your Belief System

In order for you to function in your purpose in life, you must have a clear understanding of your belief system. Your belief system has to do with your mindset. What type of information are you feeding yourself? Your mind absorbs whatever you feed it, negatively or positively. If in your thoughts, all you see in the world is darkness, consciously or subconsciously, it will magnify in your intellect, and project in your belief system which can be experienced in the physical realm. In other words, your belief system starts in the spiritual realm. And whatever exists in the spiritual realm, will eventually actualize in the physical.

Therefore, you have to decide, whose side are you on, God, or Devil? Light or darkness? Your belief system, or your mindset is generated from your accumulative thoughts, and what you're open to hearing. For instance, if you consistently look at a tree and you tell yourself that that tree is your god. Or, you frequently listen to someone telling you, you need that tree to survive. Your subconscious mind will first grasp the theory; which will eventually manifest in your consciousness.

Similarly, when you study and understand the word of God, what He declares about you, and you take the bull by the horn, meaning literarily applying them into your life, it will work for you. For example, His word says that "no weapon fashioned against you shall prosper." If you literarily hold on to this statement and apply it in your life without any atom of doubt in your heart, it will automatically become a shield of protection in your life. In other words, His holy word becomes alive, and a repellant to every evil forces that comes against you.

Also, you must decide not to get stuck in the past, where you used to be. Leave your past errors where they belong in the past; and move forward with the grace of God. Don't allow your tragedies of the past to define you and your future. Keep pressing forward as apostle Paul admonished, because our only hope is Jesus Christ, who satisfies us with fresh living water.

Only glance at your past to live better today; but, gaze at your future, believing it is brighter; for there lies your destiny in Jesus Christ.

You Must Choose To Live Without Fear And Doubt

Living without fear and doubt, is easier said than done. I was listening to Pastor Mark Finley one day, and he made a statement that, "when Jesus impresses you to do something, do not delay." I immediately felt like he was talking directly to me, because many times in the past, I found myself struggling with what ought to be a simple decision. To say yes is a simple thing to do. But when we apply our human logic to a situation we don't understand, our human logic tells us that the situation could not be right, hence, we struggle in deciding what to do.

My old self would sit and analyze the why of the message, and the what ifs. The human logic would start pointing out the perceptions of the religious people about the issue, and sometimes I'd even hear their voices in my head, revealing their disappointment on my side supporting the message. But, thank God, He always comes through for me whenever I find myself in such dilemma. This was me until I prayed to God to help me to obey Him always, whether it makes sense to me or not. Afterall, it's not about me, but it's all about Him. Human perception of me should not prevent me from obeying my Father. I know my Father's voice; therefore, I must heed to His voice. Man, I should respect, but God, I must obey at all times. Well, I'm still a working progress. But, one thing I know for sure, is this: the expectation of me, by my Lord, my Father-God, supersedes human expectations of me. And no human declaration over my life equates nor can it override the declaration of my heavenly Father for my life.

Why do we over analyze the illogical? It's because of the fear of the unknown. And the fear of the unknown produces doubt in our minds. Your strong belief in God will help you to neutralize fear and doubt from your system. In David, the shepherd boy's story, ended in victory because of his connection to God. He had faith in what he declared that God would do for him. And so, it was.

Your Belief must supersede Your Logic
Fly On Trust Zone

A good example where belief supersedes logic is the lepers' story, in 2 kings 7. There was a great famine in the land of Samaria; because the King of Aram had mobilized his entire army to lay a siege to Samaria, against the Israelites. The famine was so severe that the King of Israel decided to pay Elisha a visit concerning the hardship and hunger in the Land, because he felt what was happening was the hand of God upon them.

The king then sent his right-hand man servant first to Elisha the Prophet; upon arrival, the messenger from the king said to Elisha, "The king said, This disaster is from the Lord. Why should I wait for the Lord any longer?"

And Prophet Elisha replied, "Hear the word of the Lord. This is what the Lord says: About this time tomorrow, a seah of the finest flower will sell for a shekel and two seahs of barley for a shekel at the gate of Samaria." Guess what was the response of the officer, whom the king trusted to send to Elisha? He was filled with unbelief, because what the Prophet said was illogical to the human mind. So, he replied, "Look, even if the Lord should open the floodgates of the heavens, could this happen?"

His human logic could not comprehend to imagine the miracle Elisha was talking about. Can you blame him? There has been scarcity of food in the land of Samaria for such a long time that some women resorted to eating their own children. (2Kings 6: 28,29). This was what pushed the king to the edge, why he decided to go to Elisha with the query.

When the messenger spoke to Elisha with disbelief, Elisha responded to his question: "You will see it with your own eyes, but you will not eat any of it!" This sounds scary.

The Lepers' Risk

At the time of the famine, "there were four men with leprosy at the entrance of the city gate." And they asked each other, should we sit right here and die? If we say, let's go to the city, in the midst of the famine, we will die of starvation. But, if we stay here, we will still die. Therefore, they decided to go to the camp of the Arameans to surrender. "If they spare us, we live; if they kill us, then we die." Wow! There was risk all round. They had three possibilities, and all could result in them dying. However, they had to decide, in spite of all odds, they had to choose one out of the three options. After all considerations, they had to choose the possibility that had a glimpse of hope, trusting God that the outcome would be favorable.

When it was sundown, the Lepers set out on their

journey to the Arameans' camp to surrender; hoping they'd spear their lives. Lo, and behold, as they arrived at the beginning of the camp, they saw no one, they went further in, there was not a soul in the camp; it was like a ghost town.

What happened to the Arameans' armies?

The God that does wonders for His people showed up in a mighty way. What happened is this: at the time the lepers left the city gate, their station to head out to the Arameans' camp, by the Lord's doing, the Arameans armies, heard "the sound of chariots and horses, and a great army," and they said to one another, "Look, the king of Israel has hired the Hittite and the Egyptian Kings to attack us!" As a result, they abandoned all their properties and ran for their lives. This happened about the same time the lepers left their station at the city gate. "They left the camp as it was and ran for their lives. Amazing!

What can the Lord not do for those He loves?

When the Lepers walked to the end of the camps, and saw no one, no Aramean army, they entered one of the tents, ate, drank, and carried some goods: silver, gold and clothes; they went and hid them. They went back, entered another tent, and did the same thing. Suddenly, they realized, what they were doing was not right, they should not keep the good news to themselves; and, they are not to wait till daylight, so they'd not be punished. Therefore, they proceeded to the palace at once to share the good news.

They went to the city gate keepers to divulge the news. The gate keepers spread the news in the palace.

The King's Disbelief

The King got up in the middle of the night and summoned his officers and said, "I will tell you what the Arameans have done to us. They know we are starving; so, they have left the camp to hide in the countryside thinking, They will surely come out, and then we will take them alive and get into the city." This was the king's assumption; he was enveloped with fear. Human logic convinced his mindset to disbelief the fact. His judgement was crowded with doubt.

Fortunately, one of his officers suggested, he should ask some of his men to take five horses and go for raking, to survey the camp environment; to get to the root of the matter. When the messengers returned, they reported, that all they saw were the Arameans' properties scattered on the road way; things they dumped on the way as they were running for their lives. As a result, the people of Samaria, rushed into the camp to loot the Arameans commodities.

Elisha's prophecy came to pass; "a seah of the finest flour sold for a shekel, and two seahs of barley sold for a shekel, as the Lord had said." It happened that the king's right-hand man was positioned at the gate to oversee the affairs of food distribution and sales. In the process, the people rioted and trampled on him, and he died; just like Elisha prophesied, that he would see the abundance of food with his eyes; but would not eat any. This was a result of his disbelief; he doubted God.

What are the important lessons learned from this story?

- It's very vital to always trust God; be obedient to His word. The king's right-hand messenger died, because he valued his human logic over 'thus says the Lord.'

- Having faith alone is not enough without action. Action, is taking risks, believing that God will work it out; even when you don't know how. For the fact that the lepers decided to take the risk, God showed up; he gave them a miracle that they never imagined. This is an example of what I mean by 'work your faith'.

- God may not answer your prayers according to your wishes, but He will answer according to His Will for you. Even though God did not heal them of their leprosy disease, He surprised them with a bigger miracle. He speared their lives and sustained them. They also had the privilege of becoming the good news bearers to their people.

- We learned from the king's disbelief, that fear and doubt can take away your joy. And when you live in fear, you can deprive yourself of God's blessings. Therefore, go beyond faith; ride on trust zone. In the story of Joseph, in spite of his circumstances, he never wavered; he trusted God the whole time. And God showed up and exalted him mightily.

In a nutshell, history and experience have taught us that the prerequisite to your miracle is taking the risk that is steering at your face. We've discovered that miracles aren't just activated by faith; they are activated by making a decision beyond human logic, and taking action. In other words, miracles are experienced by those who are willing to make the first move. And certainly, the Almighty God will make a mighty move on their behalf, like he did for the lepers. "Who can battle with the Lord? I say, no body."

Everything boils down to your mind set; therefore, believe right, think right and act right.

PART SIX

Blessing The Children

Be fruitful and multiply; fill the earth and subdue it; have dominion over every living thing that moves on the earth.

"Trust in the Lord with all your heart and lean not on your own understanding; in all your ways submit to him, and he will make your paths straight." Proverbs 3: 5,6 NIV.

CHAPTER ELEVEN

My Beloved

My beloved,
I give you today, the ladder staff of God's promises, a symbol of God's covenant with you....
For every situation, stand on His promises.
Wherever you are, wherever you go, His presence is always with you.
His DNA runs through your blood.
As your body is a temple of God, the Holy Spirit.
Hold on to the word of God; it is your wisdom.
Remember to always follow the Good Shepherd–Jesus Christ.
He is the light of your path.
Thank you for accepting me as your friend all these years without undermining my status—as your mother.
Remember, the word of God is your wisdom.
Through His love comes an overflow of showers of blessing upon you.
Therefore, I pray, our Father-God bless you and keep you.
And let His face shine upon you and give you peace.
Let Him be gracious unto you, now and always.
In Jesus' Name.
Amen.

But now in Christ Jesus you who once were far away have been brought near by the blood of Christ. Ephesians 2:13. NIV

Chapter 11: My Beloved

> *The Spirit himself testifies with our spirit that we are God's children. Now if we are children, then we are heirs—heirs of God and co heirs with Christ, if indeed we share in his sufferings in order that we may also share in his glory. Romans 8:16,17 NIV.*

Hope!
Hope does not disappoint

My beloved, I present to you: HOPE!
Never let go of hope.
Hope wins all the time.

Learning from past mistakes is how you find the strength to move forward.
Allowing hope to take you to the future will become your victory;
because belief is your stepping stone to be able to see through eyes of faith.
Faith will aide you to envision your destination according to the promises of God.
Therefore beloved, make sure you never lose hope in life, no matter what!
Jesus gave you hope and victory, to conquer failure, ill health, disappointments, sadness, and poverty.
Look up to hope; may the light of success be brighter in your future.

Now Hope does not disappoint, because the love of God has been poured out in our hearts by the Holy Spirit who was given to us. Romans 5:5 NKJV

Blessed are those whose help is the God of Jacob whose hope is in the LORD their God.
Psalm 46:5 NIV.

Therefore brethren, "Let us hold fast the confession of our hope without wavering, for He who promised is faithful." Hebrews 10: 23 NKJV.

Faith
Without faith, it is impossible to please God

Beloved, hold on to Faith.
Faith is the road map to your destiny.
He will never mislead you;
Never lose faith no matter how large the crowd is.
No matter where you find yourself,
look for the light of God that trails faith and follow it.
It will connect you to God's favors, and great successes.

Therefore, having been justified by faith, we have peace with God through our Lord Jesus Christ, through whom also we have access by faith into this grace in which we stand, and rejoice in hope of the glory of God.

Chapter 11: My Beloved

And not only that, but we also glory in tribulations, knowing that tribulation produces perseverance; and perseverance character; and character hope.
Romans 5:1-4. NKJV

Now faith is confidence in what we hope for and assurance about what we do not see.... And without faith it is impossible to please God because anyone who comes to him must believe that he exists and that he rewards those who earnestly seek him. Hebrews 11: 1, 6. NIV

By the grace of God, we are saved through faith. With faith comes obedience to God's instructions. For example, God told Noah to build an Ark to save him, his family and two of each species of all the creatures on the Earth; when God decided to destroy the world with flood because of the wickedness of the people. Noah obeyed because he had faith in God, even when he could not logically comprehend the idea. He was not discouraged, even when other people thought of him as a mentally deranged human being, for the fact that the idea of God destroying the whole earth with flood was not logical to the human mind.

Also, When God told Abraham to leave his home, a place where everybody knew him by name and directed him to go to a foreign Country, where he'd become a stranger living in tents. He did not hesitate, but obeyed God because he had faith in God. Abraham trusted God completely, without knowing where he was going. He left his home and moved to a strange, but God's Promised Land.

For he was looking forward to the city with foundations, whose architect and builder is God. Hebrews 11:10. NIV

When I say Abraham did not hesitate, but obeyed God, I'm not saying, or even implying that he had no concerns. I believe as a human being, he must have struggled a little with the idea before he decided. But, Abraham as a faithful man of God, anchored on God's promise, and he acted. He packed his belongings, his family, and proceeded on a journey to the unknown because he trusted the Almighty God, for their guidance, protection, and provision.

In a nutshell, faith is our acceptance of the grace of God, our confidence on His promises, and our reliance upon His goodness—total dependence on God.

Believe

Without belief, it is difficult to see what hope has lined up for you in the future; successes and God's favors.

When you believe, hope will cheerfully direct you to your future.

And you can envision your successful destiny through eyes of faith.

Belief introduces you to hope, who is responsible for directing you to your pathway. While faith takes you to your divine destiny. Therefore, beloved, you need belief so hope and faith can assure you victory—success in life. "Everything is possible for one who believes." Mark 9:23 NIV. May the Almighty God, grant you peace and all your heart's desires. In Jesus' Name. Amen.

"Whoever believes me, as scripture has said, rivers of living water will flow from within them." John 7: 38.NIV

Our Lord Jesus is talking about the Holy Spirit—the Spirit of God that dwells within us, that calms our heart with divine peace, and joy—rivers of living water.

Trust

Trust in the Lord forever, for the Lord, the Lord himself, is the Rock eternal. Isaiah 26:4 NIV

Never let go of your belief in God— Trust.
In a clouded day, your connection to hope through belief,
will bring sunshine to the pathway leading to your destiny.
Although hope directs you to your future, you need eyes of faith, to clearly see your way to your divine destiny.

Sometimes, the obstacles on the way may cloud your judgement,
telling you, you are on the wrong path.
This is when your experiences go contrary to what faith reveals or tells you.
When this happens, accelerate to trust, it's the only way.

Trust arrives when situations are not logical—when things are not making sense, hold on to belief.
Trust is the only spirit that will take you to where you ought to be when you can no longer see through eyes of faith.

When faith is threatened, keep riding on the Road Master – belief, until trust shows up. Look beyond faith, and trust will arrive.
Your unshaken belief in God – is trust; which is

advanced-faith beyond human comprehension.

Faith rides, therefore, it can be tempted and contaminated with doubt and fear. But trust flies. Hence, the enemy— the devil, cannot touch it, for trust is in God's territory. Remember, trust cannot arrive in the absence of belief – the road master. Therefore, my Beloved, believe! believe!! believe, and put your trust in God.

Let me take you to God's promise to Abraham becoming the father of many nations, when he was about a hundred years old and the body was already dead; also, Sarah, his wife's womb was considered dead at her age.

"He did not waver at the promise of God through unbelief, but was strengthened in faith, giving glory to God, and being fully convinced that what He had promised He was also able to perform." Romans 4: 20,21 NKJV.

Also, God asked him later to sacrifice his promised son, Isaac, yet he was obedient without question. You and I today would have said, I reject it in Jesus' name. We would have been overtaken by doubt, saying, it cannot be God. Perhaps we would say to God, are you sure of what you're saying? Remember, you promised me that I'd become the father of many nations. Have you forgotten, God. Now you want me to kill him.

What kind of love is that? I thought you love me, and you said I'm your friend. I don't understand you anymore. Papa, I don't think I can do what you're asking of me to do, kill my child that you gave me and my wife at our old age? You mean all the lamb I've been giving you is not enough for you anymore? My Father, ask me to do anything for you, and I will, but not this very one; murder my own child?

Can you imagine, if Abraham sounded like that, what would have happened? He wouldn't have known about God's provision of the ram in Genesis 2:13.

Abraham was so faithful to God he trusted Him even when the request made no sense to him. Even when his son Isaac asked him, I see everything for the sacrifice, but "where is the lamb?" He responded faithfully, "God Himself will provide the lamb for the burnt offering my son."

In summary, Trust is a type of Faith which operates at a higher bond or connectivity between your spiritual being and the God Spirit, which operates when situations are not logical to the human mind—when it doesn't make sense. At this high level of faith, fear and doubt cannot succeed in penetration, no matter the efforts of the devil. Therefore, it's extremely important to trust God always by believing in His word, even when your situation looks contrary to what God has spoken. When God says a thing, know that it must surely come to pass, no matter what and how long it might take because He's not a human being that He should lie.

May God help us to always be faithful and obedient to the command of our God. In Jesus Name. Amen. Great is the faithfulness of our God. I say to myself," *The Lord is my portion; therefore, I will wait for him."* Lamentations 3:24 NIV.

My Prayer For You

I pray this day that our God, out of His glorious riches strengthens you with power through His Spirit in your inner being, "so that Christ may dwell in your hearts through faith. And I pray that you, being rooted and established in love, may have power," (Ephesians 3:17) and the understanding of the love of God, and His grace in which we receive through the death and resurrection of the Lord Jesus Christ, our Savior. Let the grace and peace of God be with you always. In Jesus' Name. Amen.

I declare upon you, in the Mighty Name of our Lord Jesus Christ, the peace of God to reign in your life.

No weapon fashioned against you shall prosper. Wherever you find yourselves, you'll always be the head and never the tail. Opportunities will look for you. And every door of opportunity you knock, will be open for you, you'll be highly esteemed with favor, acceptance, recognition, respect, visibility, kindness, love, promotion and every good thing according to your heart's desires. Achievement and success will be synonymous with your name. Above all, I declare upon you, good health and long life. Whatever you touch will prosper, and you shall prosper. And I declare, the blessings of God upon your life, be extended to all your generations, in Jesus' Mighty Name. Amen, and amen.

Beloved, know that you have the grace of God upon your life. And you must never forget the golden rules our Lord commanded us to uphold. First, "to love the Lord your God, with all your heart, and with all your soul, and with all your strength, and with all your mind" (Luke 10:27). Second, to love your neighbors as yourself." (Mark 12:31). Therefore, my beloved, as our God blesses you, treasure being a blessing to others.

Above all, may the grace and the love of God, help everyone of us to be a watch man, and a mouthpiece for God on Earth, living right for Jesus; at the end, we shall meet in the Kingdom of God to live eternally with our Lord and King, Jesus Christ. Amen.

Safety of Abiding in the Presence of God

*He who dwells in the secret place of the Most High
Shall abide under the shadow of the Almighty.
I will say of the Lord, "He is my refuge and my fortress;
My God, in Him I will trust."*

*Surely, He shall deliver you from the snare of the fowler[a]
And from the perilous pestilence.
He shall cover you with His feathers,
And under His wings you shall take refuge;
His truth shall be your shield and buckler.*

*You shall not be afraid of the terror by night,
Nor of the arrow that flies by day,
Nor of the pestilence that walks in darkness,
Nor of the destruction that lays waste at noonday.
A thousand may fall at your side,
And ten thousand at your right hand;
But it shall not come near you.*

*Only with your eyes shall you look,
And see the reward of the wicked.
Because you have made the Lord, who is my refuge,
Even the Most High, your dwelling place,
No evil shall befall you,*

Nor shall any plague come near your dwelling;
For He shall give His angels charge over you,
To keep you in all your ways.
In their hands they shall bear you up,
Lest you dash your foot against a stone.
You shall tread upon the lion and the cobra,
The young lion and the serpent you shall trample underfoot.
"Because he has set his love upon Me, therefore I will deliver him;
I will set him on high, because he has known My name.

He shall call upon Me, and I will answer him;
I will be with him in trouble;
I will deliver him and honor him.
With long life I will satisfy him,
And show him My salvation." Amen.

Psalm 91 New King James Version (NKJV).
(Insert the appropriate gender application).

The Components of the belief system

The components of the Belief System are: Believe, Hope, Faith and Trust. Hope awakens your dream to mold the imagination of your heart desires; while faith brings your imaginations alive. Faith also gives you the confidence that your dream is achievable;

Chapter 11: My Beloved

you can envision it mentally and feel it in your spirit. But trust, has no room for failure. Trust expresses confidence, reliability, honesty and goodness.

Notably, every outcome starts with your belief system. Belief activates hope to awaken your vision or dream. Therefore, Hope is a door opener. And "Faith purifies the heart." Acts 15: 8.
In other words, belief is an activator of hope, and a projector of faith. Furthermore, the intensity in your belief system will generate trust.

People of God, know yourselves, and guard your hearts. We are instructed by the holy word of God to guard our hearts and take our thoughts captive, because every outcome in our desires of life, starts from our hearts, and the thoughts of our minds, through our belief system. Whatever your heart attracts is welcomed by your spirit being first, which will eventually manifest in the physical. Hence, it's important to believe right.

Not believing right can result to an internal battle called "the battle of the mind". This is simply the battle between good and evil within you. But, when you believe right and surrender your will to the Will of God, the God Spirit within you—the Holy Spirit, will pull you out of the enemy's generated thoughts and his evil plots against you, and therefore, give you the will power to overcome.

It does not therefore, depend on human desires or effort, but on God's mercy. For scripture says to Pharaoh: "I raised you up for this very purpose, that I might display my power in you and that my name might be proclaimed in all the earth.
Romans 9:16,17.

PART SEVEN

Acknowledge God! My Heart Sings For The Lord!

God says, "I will save those who love me and will protect those who acknowledge me as Lord. Psalm 91:14 GNT.

I will sing to the LORD all my life; I will sing praise to my God as long as I live. May my meditation be pleasing to him, as I rejoice in the LORD.
Psalm 104: 33,34 NIV

CHAPTER TWELVE

The Songs Of My Heart!

Ring Hallelujah To Our King

Saints of God come together,
Let's worship Our Lord Jesus Christ.
He who died because of our sins,
He rose from the grave,
And has gone to Heaven.
He's coming back again to take us home.
Ring, ring, ring Hallelujah to His name.
Come, and sing hosanna;
Sing Hosanna to our Lord and King.

All ye Christians come together,
To rescue the perishing of the field.
Bring them back to the Christian fold.
Our Lord commanded,
We should go to the world;
Preach His gospel and tell His people,
That our Lord Jesus is coming back again.
Say to every corner of this Earth,
Our Lord Jesus Christ is coming soon.

I Must Tell The Wonderful Story

I will live to tell that story of love;
The story of the precious blood.
I'll tell the wonderful story of Jesus,
No matter wherever I am.
I must tell the story of my Savior,
Who died on the cross for me.
He was crucified for my redemption;
Such love, I must, testify.

For God so loved the world that he gave his one and only son, that whoever believes in him shall not perish but have eternal life. John 3:16 NIV.

Without Jesus, Where Would I Be Today?

Without Jesus, where would I be today?
Take my hand Lord,
For I cannot stand without You.
Let my spirit being move according to your Will.
Move my physical being to harmonize
with my spirit, that all of me,
will continually submerge in your presence.
Let your tranquil peace and love
harmonize my heart, soul, mind and strength;
To mirror You, Lord, I pray.

I wonder where I would be
Without my Savior Jesus.
He took me the way I was,
And made me the way I should be.
Thank you, my Lord Savior Jesus,
You're able to carry me through.
My desire is to live for You forever;
Let Your righteous presence envelop me.
Without my Lord, and Savior Jesus,
Where would I be today?

Song of God's Majesty and Love
A Praise of David.

I will extol You, my God, O King;
And I will bless Your name forever and ever.
Every day I will bless You,
And I will praise Your name forever and ever.

Great is the Lord, and greatly to be praised;
And His greatness is unsearchable.
One generation shall praise Your works to another,
And shall declare Your mighty acts.

I[a] will meditate on the glorious splendor of Your majesty,
And on Your wondrous works. [b]
Men shall speak of the might of Your awesome acts,
And I will declare Your greatness.
They shall utter the memory of Your great goodness,
And shall sing of Your righteousness.

The Lord is gracious and full of compassion,
Slow to anger and great in mercy.
The Lord is good to all,
And His tender mercies are over all His works.

All Your works shall praise You, O Lord,
And Your saints shall bless You.

They shall speak of the glory of Your kingdom,
And talk of Your power,
To make known to the sons of men His mighty acts,
And the glorious majesty of His kingdom.
Your kingdom is an everlasting kingdom,
And Your dominion endures throughout all generations. [c]
The Lord upholds all who fall,
And raises up all who are bowed down.
The eyes of all look expectantly to You,
And You give them their food in due season.

You open Your hand
And satisfy the desire of every living thing.
The Lord is righteous in all His ways,
Gracious in all His works.
The Lord is near to all who call upon Him,
To all who call upon Him in truth.
He will fulfill the desire of those who fear Him;
He also will hear their cry and save them.

The Lord preserves all who love Him,
But all the wicked He will destroy.
My mouth shall speak the praise of the Lord,
And all flesh shall bless His holy name
Forever and ever. Amen.
Psalm 145 New King James Version (NKJV).

Standing on the Promises
R. Kelso Carter, S (1849-1928) SDAH 518

1
Standing on the promises of Christ my King,
Thru eternal ages let His praises ring;
Glory in the highest I will shout and sing,
Standing on the promises of God.
Refrain
Standing, standing,
Standing on the promises
of God my Savior;
Standing, standing,
I'm standing on the promises of God.

2
Standing on the promises that cannot fail,
When the howling storms of doubt and fear assail,
By the living word of God I shall prevail,
Standing on the promises of God.

3
Standing on the promises of Christ the Lord,
Bound to Him eternally by love's strong cord,
Overcoming daily with the Spirit's sword,
Standing on the promises of God.

by Johnson Oatman Jr. (1856-1922)

1
In the blood from the cross,
I have been washed from sin;
But to be free from dross,
Still I would enter in.
Refrain
Deeper yet, deeper yet,
Into the crimson flood;
Deeper yet, deeper yet,
Under the precious blood.

2
Day by day, hour by hour,
Blessings are sent to me;
But for more of His power,
Ever my prayer shall be.

3
Near to Christ I would live,
Following Him each day;
What I ask He will give;
So then with faith I pray.

4

Now I have peace, sweet peace,
While in this world of sin;
But to pray I'll not cease
Till I am pure within.

He Lives SDAH 251

by Alfred H. Ackley, 1933

I serve a risen Savior,
He's in the world today;
I know that He is living,
whatever men may say;
I see His hand of mercy,
I hear His voice of cheer
And just the time
I need Him He's always near.
Refrain
He lives, He lives,
Christ Jesus lives today!
He walks with me
and talks with me
along life's narrow way.
He lives, He lives,
salvation to impart!
You ask me how I know He lives?
He lives within my heart.

2.
In all the world around me
I see His loving care,
And tho' my heart grows weary
I never will despair;
I know that He is leading

thru all the stormy blast,
The day of His appearing
will come at last.

3
Rejoice, rejoice, O Christian,
lift up your voice and sing, Eternal hallelujahs
to Jesus Christ the King!
The hope of all who seek Him,
the help of all who find,
None other is so loving,
so good and kind

My Hope Is Built on Nothing Less

Edward Mote 1834(1797-1874) SDAH 522

My hope is built on nothing less
Than Jesus' blood and righteousness.
I dare not trust the sweetest frame,
But wholly lean on Jesus' name.
Refrain
On Christ the solid rock I stand;
All other ground is sinking sand,
All other ground is sinking sand.

2
When Darkness veils His lovely face,
I rest on His unchanging grace.
In every high and stormy gale,
My anchor holds within the veil.

3
His oath, His covenant, His blood
Supports me in the whelming flood.
When all around my soul gives way,
He then is all my hope and stay.

4
When He shall come with trumpet sound,
O may I then in Him be found!
Dressed in His righteousness alone,
Faultless to stand before the throne.

CHAPTER THIRTEEN

The Bottom Line

It's Not Over Until God Says It's Over

It's not over until God says it's over!
I am created by my heavenly Father.
I came to this world not by accident.
He designed my life just right,
To serve my purpose on Earth.
I say the devil has no right to touch my life.
Get thee behind me Satan,
You have no right! No right to my life.
I am covered with the blood of Jesus Christ.

Heaven declares war against my enemies.
Touch not my anointed my God declares.
He designed every step of my life pathway.
He sent His beloved son to wash away my sins.
Every day I live and feel gloriously and victoriously.
Thank You Father, for sending me to planet Earth.
I'll see You at the end of my assignment on Earth.
Heaven! Heaven is my permanent home.
I love You oh Lord, my All.

Chapter 13: The bottom line

Why You Must Be Both Responsible and Accountable For Your Life

Some people may say, they have always lived a responsible life. Alright! You are responsible, are you accountable? You can be responsible for a thing, for example, you're a minister in the Lord's vineyard, every arm of the ministry reports to you because you are responsible in the overall affairs of that ministry.

However, the individual department heads or officers reporting to you are accountable for their specific assignments.

But, if something goes wrong because of what they do, you, the overseer is responsible for the action. It is your reputation that will be on the line because you're responsible for the organization. The individual can be disciplined within the organization for the fact that he/she was accountable for the action, but it does not relieve you from the responsibility of that action.

Hence, responsibility means, you have the power and the authority to control the outcome of a situation, or answerable, or eligible to defend.

On the other hand, accountability lies on individuals. No other can account for you, you have to account for yourself.

In matters of life, every human being that is up to the age of differentiating right from wrong, is both responsible and accountable for his/her life. On the last day, when our Lord shall come, all human will be answerable to God. You will give account to God how you lived the life he gave to you. You will report on the assignment He gave you to accomplish in your lifetime. All the opportunities He provided for you will be accounted for.

Beloved of God, don't you think it's high time you opened your heart for the truth, embrace it, and live it? Now you know, your identity is a child, daughter/son of an Almighty God. You now know how to discern your mission on earth, and with the direction of the Holy Spirit, your accomplishment is assured. You can define what life means to you. And especially, you're aware that the only life building that can stand the test of time is the foundation laid on Jesus Christ, our Redeemer, Lord, and Savior. Do not delay; tomorrow may be too late. Start living a life of accountability right here and now.

Finally, when you are doing that which God sent you here on planet earth to do, that is your destiny. Be responsible, hold on to it and protect it with the power and authority given you at the cross of Calvary, by the risen Savior. He conquered, so we will remain victorious forever. No more excuses, you have the power and authority over the great liar, the old serpent, the devil. Focus on the Lord, hearken to the voice of God, and crush Satan under your feet. Declare and proclaim the joy-filled life you want to live, and your kingdom of heaven starts on earth right now. God designed a beautiful world with everything His children need and want and gave us the key. Utilize that power and authority. You are no longer a slave, you're free. Make that known to the devil, through your actions.

Live a life of expectancy; no matter what the enemy dishes out, tell yourself, I refuse to be a victim, because I am victorious. Make declaration to move forward in spite of.... Say these to yourself, "I am the righteousness of God; I am the apple of His eyes; I am not born with the spirit of doubt and fear, but of love and a sound mind. I must live and not die; no weapon fashioned against me shall prosper." And I must live to fulfill my destiny.

Recognize your gifts and talents, and develop them. Have some drives; be passionate about living; be persistent in carrying on with your mission; and be focused on achieving your dream. In all, be a force in your generation; leave a legacy. At the down of the sun, take account of your life, how meaningful have you lived? Will you be in a position to say to our Lord: "I fought the good fight and I finished the race," like apostle Paul?

For our citizenship is in heaven, from which we also eagerly wait for the Savior, the Lord Jesus Christ, who will transform our lowly body that it may be conformed to His glorious body, according to the working by which He is able even to subdue all things to Himself.
Philippians 3:20,21.NKJV.

Conclusion

Children of God use this book as a companion in your journey of life to your destiny. Never give up on your dreams. As I rightly stated in my book—*My Pledge! The power of prayer* "Make your dream big enough for God to use and enlarge for His purpose." Do not share your dreams with the little minds—those that will deposit fear and doubt, in your spirit. Identify your mission on Earth, then move on to accomplishing it. However, if you're still not sure of what it is, then ask God for clarity. He will do more than give you your life specifications, which were prepared before your existence on Earth. But start by searching through the instructional manual—the Holy Book of Life {the Bible}, which He has given to us to direct our paths.

No matter the perception of people or what they say about you, if your aspiration is to live right by God, no enemy can damage your image in the eyes of God. If you know your identity as a child of God, you'll know not to focus on the negative forces around you, because you're not of this world; you're here just for a little while, to go about our Father's business. Therefore, the world does not define who you are. When you're solid in the Lord, devil and his agents will never succeed in pulling your legs off the ground. Know that you are in the palm of the Most-High God, where nobody can snatch you away. Be like "A Moving Train"— be focused. Keep your eyes upon Jesus, and all will be well with you because, victory is only in Jesus Christ, our strength, and our solid foundation.

In addition, keep on loving; love God, love others, and love yourself.

Finally, have a grateful heart. Honor your creator, glorify Him with thanksgiving. In other words, testimony of the Lord's goodness should never depart from your mouth.

To God be the glory!

Discover Your Coat of Many Colors

Biblical References:

Ephesians 2:13 NIV, 3:17
Romans 8: 16,17 NIV
Romans 5:5 NKJV
Romans 5:1—4 NKJV
John 7: 38 NIV
Isaiah 26: 4 NIV
Romans 4: 20,21 NKJV
Genesis 22:13
Lamentations 3: 24 NIV
Proverbs 3:5,6 NIV

Acts 15:8
Romans 8: 8-11 NKJV
Psalm 143: 9-10 inspired
Proverbs 3:5,6 NKJV
Philippians 4:13 NKJV
Jeremiah 1:4-10. NIV
Psalm35:1, 3; Psalm 61 inspired
Psalm 91 NKJV
Genesis 1: 1, 3-5 NIV
Psalm 146:5 NIV
Revelation 22: 17 NIV
Psalm 145 NKJV, 146:1,2
John 3:16 NIV
Revelation 22:20,21. NKJV
Psalm 146 NKJV, 34:7 NIV
Hebrew 11:10 NIV
Mark 9:23 NIV, 12:31 NIV
John 1: 1-3
Genesis 1: 26-28, 39:1-5
1Samuel 17
1Samuel 16:14
Psalm 34:4 NKJV
Revelation 22:20,21
Jeremiah 29:11,12
Jeremiah 1: 11 NIV
John 3:16,17 NJKV
Revelation 1:5,6 NKJV

Revelation 5:9,10 NKJV
Ecclesiastes 10:20
Psalm 33:18-22 NIV, 34:4 NKJV
Acts 4:29-31NKJV
Psalms 46: 5 NIV
Hebrews 10:23NKJV; 1:1,6 NIV
Luke 10:27 NIV
2 kings 6 & 7 NIV
Genesis 1: 1,2 NKJV
1 Peter 1: 3-9 ESV
Romans 8: 28-31 NKJV
Psalm 105: 1-24NKJV
Joshua 1: 9 GNT
2 Chronicles 20: 15-20 Inspired
Matthew 7: 24-27 NLT
Proverbs 3: 5,6 NIV
Psalm 9 :14 GNT
Psalm 104: 33, 34 NIV
2 Timothy 1: 7 NKJV
Philippians 3: 20, 21 NKJV
Matthew 7:7 NKJV
Romans 8:8-11 NKJV

HYMNS OF PRAISE
S D A H 518, 302, 251, 522

NOTE: Endeavor to get my book, "MY PLEDGE! for study companion. There are topics I covered there that will aid you in the understanding of the subject: life's journey, purpose, and how to use the power within you. Also, how to hear God, and how to ask (effective prayer), through real life testimonies. God is still speaking today.

About The Author

Fyne C. Ogonor is an entrepreneur, educator, inspirational Speaker, Trainer, a Philanthropist, business Consultant to Change Makers, author and a song writer. She's also a Spiritual Counsellor through her prayer ministry.

Her other books include:

A Moving Train

My Pledge! The power of prayer

Baby Eagle And The Chicks: The Similarity Between Tom and The Baby Eagle

Baby Eagle And the Chicks For Kindergarten And Preschoolers

And coming soon: "The Best Gift Ever! A letter from God at Christmas"

www.ingramcontent.com/pod-product-compliance
Lightning Source LLC
Chambersburg PA
CBHW071913110526
44591CB00011B/1666